sex
sushi
& salvation

sex
sushi
& salvation

thoughts on intimacy, community, & eternity

CHRISTIAN GEORGE

moody publishers
chicago

All Scripture quotations, unless otherwise indicated, are from *The Message*, copyright © by Eugene H. Peterson 1993, 1994, 1995. Used by permission of NavPress Publishing Group.

Scripture quotations marked NIV are taken from the *Holy Bible, New International Version*.® NIV.® Copyright © 1973, 1978, 1984 by International Bible Society. Used by permission of Zondervan. All rights reserved.

Cover Designer: Kirk DouPonce, DogEared Design
Cover Image: iStockphoto.com
Interior Design: Smartt Guys design
Editor: Jim Vincent

Library of Congress Cataloging-in-Publication Data

George, Christian Timothy, 1981-
 Sex, sushi & salvation : thoughts on intimacy, community, and eternity/
Christian George.
    p. cm.
 Includes bibliographical references.
 ISBN 978-0-8024-8254-9
 1. Spirituality. I. Title. II. Title: Sex, sushi, and salvation.
BV4501.3.G463 2008
242--dc22
                    2007034674

ISBN: 0-8024-8254-6
ISBN-13: 978-0-8024-8254-9

We hope you enjoy this book from Moody Publishers. Our goal is to provide high-quality, thought-provoking books and products that connect truth to your real needs and challenges. For more information on other books and products written and produced from a biblical perspective, go to www.moodypublishers.com or write to:

Moody Publishers
820 N. LaSalle Boulevard
Chicago, IL 60610

1 3 5 7 9 10 8 6 4 2

Printed in the United States of America

For Rebecca,
my baby back rib

contents

When once you have tasted flight, you will forever walk the earth with your eyes turned skyward.

—LEONARDO DA VINCI

fasten your
seat belts

IT WAS A bumpy takeoff—the kind that makes atheists pray like Catholic schoolgirls.

"Please fasten your safety belts," the flight attendant requested, "and return your seat backs and tray tables to their full upright and locked positions."

Happily I obeyed. Then I looked out the airplane window as we began to move. Seventy, eighty, ninety miles an hour. We passed the point of no return, the runway was running out, and the only way back down was up. *God, have mercy.*

"I wish they would give us more peanuts," the man grumbled beside me. His lips were oily from the peanut package, but he continued stuffing his mouth. This guy was nervous.

"Not a fan of flying?" I asked, sliding my peanuts onto his tray.

He shook his head. "They say it's more dangerous to drive, but I'd rather die in a car crash than a plane crash."

He had a point.

The man consumed the poor nuts. They didn't have a snowball's chance of survival on a hot Alabama afternoon. I tried not to gag, but the urge was overwhelming. Perhaps the *Sky Mall* magazine would take my mind off the salty genocide.

It worked. There were gadgets and gizmos galore! Revolving tie racks, virtual-reality headsets, and pens that did anything and everything but write. The watches were altimeters, the sunglasses were radios, and the only thing longer than the glow-in-the-dark Slip 'n Slide was the triple-digit price tag plastered to its picture. There was even a machine to warm a roll of toilet paper before using it. *Nice.*

Suddenly, the plane jolted. It wasn't a small quiver of the wings; it was a three-second plunge into the depths. My soul sank into my stomach as I clinched the sides of my seat. "OK, God, I'm sorry for my sins."

Bump. Bump. Bump.

The man beside me was beside himself. He had finished eating my peanuts and was looking for something else to devour. I scooted closer to the window to resume my reading.

Another drop in altitude.

Luggage bins burst open, and white clouds absorbed the wing outside. I wanted to drop to my knees in prayer but wasn't about to unbuckle the seat belt. Babies screamed, children cried, and even the flight attendants were wide-eyed. I bit my lip and continued flipping through the *Sky Mall* magazine. *Look at that! An indoor/outdoor s'more maker fully equipped with marshmallows, chocolate bars, sterno, and . . .*

Bump. Bump. Bump.

I cringed. "OK, God, when I was six, I poured blue ink all over my parents' brand-new carpet. Instead of telling them, I emptied a bucket of white paint over the stains. And when I was twelve, I almost burned down our house by throwing an aerosol deodorant can into the fireplace. God, give this turbulence a Tums and land us safely on the ground!"

To my left, a woman immersed herself in a romance novel. I stole a glimpse. "Ronan wrapped his rippled arms around her waist and pulled her close. Helga trembled with lust. But she knew she could never love a Viking."

I pulled my eyes away from the book. Ancient Chinese monks believed that people only have a certain number of breaths to breathe in a lifetime. Once those breaths are used, the person dies. That's one reason they practiced meditation and other arts that slow the lungs down to increase the life span. I tried breathing slowly, but it didn't work because I was distracted by the woman beside me and her rapidly increasing breath.

"Helga felt her lips betray her as she snuggled against the warm marble of Ronan's chest."

The seat belt sign flashed, but I jumped up and darted to the bathroom. Anything to get away from Ronan's rippled body. The bathroom smelled of rotten eggs. Soap was smeared across the makeshift sink, and the last person didn't bother to flush. I ended up losing my footing, crashing against the mirror, and waiting for the turbulence to quit before I returned to my seat.

Yet this was my life. Turbulence was a frequent phenomenon for a dorky kid like me in middle school. My voice was cracking, my hormones raging, and life was a cloud I never thought would pass. Pre-algebra ate my lunch, biology molested my GPA, and a persistent cough shattered my dreams of staying in shape. Art interested me, but I always feared the artist's outcome—living from painting to painting, driving a rainbow-colored Volkswagen, and dying from exposure to oils. On top of it all I had to get braces, which made my mouth a talk-ing chain-link fence.

Closing my eyes, I opened the bathroom door and walked to my seat. My faithful *Sky Mall* magazine greeted me with hot-dog-bun-toasting technology and swinging hammocks. And yet, somehow these things did not satisfy me. I continued flipping the pages, trying to suck bits of comfort from the pictures, but eventually I had to stop. Did I really think that neon popcorn makers and alien coffee mugs could bring me peace? Could portable DVD players calm my nerves?

Turbulence has a way of reminding us what really matters in life. There I was, soaring at four hundred miles an hour through rainstorms and rolling thunder in a plane that was susceptible to lightning strikes and engine malfunction. Did I really think that *Sky Mall* magazine could mask my misery? What happens when life gets bumpy? When the letter reads, "I want out of this relationship." When the doctor says, "There's nothing else I can do for you." What then? Can salty peanuts prevent our pain? It's simple to say we're Christians when exams are easy, bills are paid, and all seems right in the world. But when the storms twist our exclamation points into question marks, we discover that there's more to life than computerized slippers and sexy ring tones. We discover that the world revolves around some-thing greater than ourselves.

Since humans are made in the image of God, we have three ba-sic passions—intimacy, community, and eternity. We burn for them, save for them, pay for them, and pray for them. But only the God who fulfills these desires within Himself can perfectly fulfill them in us. This is a book about sex, sushi, and salvation—a book of snapshots— the ups and downs, the failures and fortunes, the smiles and trials. In these chapters, I retrace my travels around the world, from pagan temples in Greece to Transylvanian mountains in Romania. I confess my lust and love, my struggle with truth, and my quest for Christ.

Fasten your seat belt. It's going to be a wild ride. And along the way we just might discover that the God who satisfies us with Himself joins us for the journey.

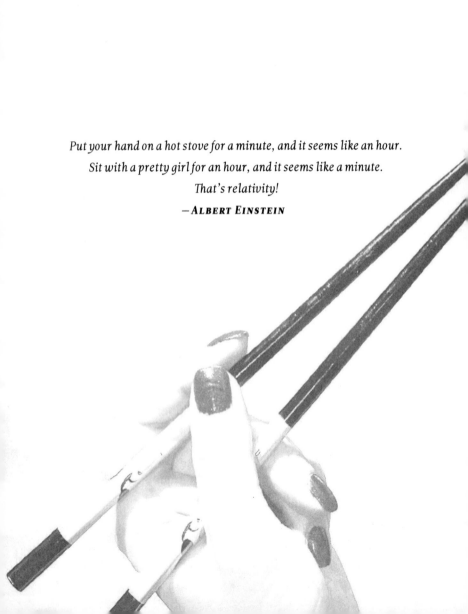

Put your hand on a hot stove for a minute, and it seems like an hour.

Sit with a pretty girl for an hour, and it seems like a minute.

That's relativity!

—ALBERT EINSTEIN

russian sex
and
wedding vows

ANYTHING was possible before God created the cosmos. Stars could have burned green instead of white. Planets could have grown like grass in the galaxy. Oceans could have oozed of Milk Duds and caramel. The whole world, in fact, could have been a trampoline, bouncing creatures across the continents.

But God had other plans. He created a universe that was hospitable for humanity—warm sunshine, fresh oxygen, flowing water. He spoke birds and beasts into being. He invented dragonflies, crocodiles, and water lilies. But something was missing. The lions didn't look like God. The tigers didn't talk like God.

"Let us make man in our image," God said (Genesis 1:26 NIV). "All in favor, raise your hand." Since God is one-in-three and three-in-one, a single hand streaked the sky, signaling a unanimous yes. Then God reached into the blackness of time, grabbed hold of nothing, decided it should become something, and altered just about every-thing so that one day He could bless it with anything. And He named it Adam, and gave him Eve.

I met my Eve on a Sunday. For many it was a day of rest, but for me, activity was in the air. The girl of my dreams was twelve feet away, and my work was certainly cut out for me. We were in the college cafeteria. The smell of burgers filled the air, but I was too nervous to notice. The rest of my life depended on this moment. I had to make it count.

My mission was simple but serious, and with great suaveness, I surveyed the scene. Every time she brought that sandwich to her mouth, I envied the turkey on her lips. What's a guy to do? Sure, I had dated before, but never a specimen like this. She was way out of my league. The brunettes of my past were brushed aside; the redheads were washed away. All the proms, dances, and dates dissolved in my mind, and there I was, captivated by this blonde before me.

"So, tell me your life story," I said, sitting down at her table. It was a risky move but a sexy one.

She looked at me with neutral eyes. But then she smiled. It was a smile to replace the millions I'd seen before, a smile that dulled the sting of yesterday's D on an English quiz.

"My name's Rebecca," she said, twisting a strand of hair around her finger. "What's yours?"

I paused as the amnesia set in. Ever since my infancy I've known my name. I've said it and spelled it a thousand times. But as I watched her caress those locks, my brain was void of thought.

"Uh, Christian," I remembered. Of course, I could have been a Brandon, Steve, or Jason if I thought it would help.

"Christian," she mused, "I like that."

It was a perfect moment, a moment carved forever in my mind. It was a moment that split my B.C. from my A.D., and over the following weeks, Rebecca took my life in a new and exciting direction. She told me about her childhood, when ice cream trucks and swimming pools occupied her hours. She told me about her greatest fear: dangling her feet over a shark-infested sea. She told me about her faith—a stubborn, risky, rugged faith that was bold enough to tell God what she thought of Him. We talked philosophy and theology, history and science. And as I turned the pages of her life, I knew she was a book worth wrapping my mind around, and hopefully one day my arms.

EMBRACE, ENGAGE, AND SURRENDER

According to the Westminster Shorter Catechism, the chief end of man is to glorify God and enjoy Him forever. God told the prophet Jeremiah, "Before I shaped you in the womb, I knew all about you" (Jeremiah 1:5). Interestingly enough, in this sense, the Hebrew word for "know" means more than cerebral awareness; it can mean sex. In Genesis 4:1, Adam *knew* his wife and she conceived a baby named Cain. To know God is to be intimate with Him. A first-base relationship is not enough. A faith that flirts cannot satisfy a God who loves. We must embrace Him, engage Him, and surrender to His will.

Salvation is like a sneeze—we can't resist it for long. Oh sure, we can delay it, swallow it, or maybe pretend that it doesn't exist. But when Christ looks across the lunch table and asks us our story, it's only a matter of time before we realize He's been tickling our nose the whole time. And He's already written an ending with us in His arms.

Spending time in the presence of Christ should not be a boring date filled with awkward pauses and early curfews; rather, it should be an exciting event, climaxing with sparks flying and passions peaking. The Creator of the universe seeks intimacy with His creation, and if the Westminster Shorter Catechism is correct and God is our chief desire, intimacy with the Eternal will be established.

A RUSSIAN REQUEST

A prostitute tried to have sex with me once. Her name was Nadia, and she lived in Russia. I was on a team of about twenty, some less experienced with mission trips than others, but all of us were committed to the project we were working on. We had come to minister to the orphans, the lowest of the low. There were hundreds of kids, most between the ages of four and fifteen. All of them had been abandoned by their parents and many abused. We had organized a summer camp where they could swim, play soccer, and learn about God. After weeks of planning and months of praying, we stepped off the bus in Vladimir, a small town near Moscow, and prepared to give these children the best summer of their lives.

Their faces were twisted with pain and rejection. Most of the girls would become prostitutes in years to come. Some would be kidnapped and trafficked to European cities for sex. Most of the boys would either serve in the military or end up in prison. And yet, as the camp progressed, so did their smiles. They began to laugh and play, and when we taught them Bible stories their eyes lit up with wild excitement. They wanted to know what happened to Joseph after he was sold into slavery. They held their breath and pretended to be Jonah, sinking beneath the surface of the sea. Some of them even did cartwheels, like the stone that rolled away from Christ's tomb.

As we were working in the camp, Nadia and I came to know one another. She worked at the camp, and her English was broken and thick. At first, it was frustrating to talk to her, like doing a Sudoku puzzle in the dark, but eventually we communicated. I told her about Alabama, how the hot summer days last from April to October. I told her of God and His grace, forgiveness, and goodness. I told her things broken people need to hear. But she also had something to say.

"Do you want to have sex with me?"

I paused.

"Do you want to have sex?" she asked again, flicking her jet-black hair away from her face.

A thousand thoughts raced through my mind. When I was in Sunday school I learned about how Joseph ran away from Potiphar's wife when she propositioned him. He didn't even stay to collect his clothes. That seemed like a good idea, and I calculated the energy it would take to hightail it out of there. But my legs did not like that option, and welded to the ground. Perhaps if I stayed, I could talk her out of it. Women like to talk, and it shouldn't be hard to turn the conversation in another direction. Even the great *Titanic* was steered by a single rudder. But then, for a brief second in time, I thought the unthinkable. It was a dark and dangerous second, but it nonetheless ticked. *What if? Who would know? Why not?*

○ ○ ○ ○ ○ ○

My first girlfriend's name was Cindy. Sure, we were in preschool, but she had skills. Really good skills. She could finger paint until the cows came home, and it was too much for me to take. I fell madly in love with her, and during naptime she consumed my little dreams. At recess we chased each other around the playground, and in class we learned to spell our names together. Cindy's mother took us out on our first "date," and it ended with chocolate ice cream all over the car.

But the relationship would have never worked out. You see, Cindy picked her nose. Granted, her fingers were exceptionally talented, but when she swirled them around in her mouth, I knew the relationship was not going to last. Besides, we were four years old. And to further complicate the situation, I was moving on to bigger and better things—kindergarten.

When I was in fifth grade, I remember sitting in a sex-education class that explained the ins and outs (quite literally) of God's great gift to humanity. Since I was the second guy in my class to grow hair on my legs, everyone looked at me to see how I would react to the naughty pictures in the textbook. Victoria's Secret wasn't a secret to me anymore, and I sat in the corner of the class and giggled. I felt like Curious George, exploring the terrain of a new and unfamiliar landscape. It was a landscape filled with colorful charts, enlightening drawings, and memorable diagrams. One page even had a pop-up chart, which gave me no small laugh. Of course, the idea of kissing a girl was foreign to me; the idea of sex, unfathomable.

Those days did change. In middle school, I all but roped the moon to snag a hug from a girl. I wrote girls letters, sent them pictures, and flirted with them in class. I laughed at their jokes, wooed them with winks, and even offered to edit their papers. Every once in a while, my squeaky, high-pitched voice gave way to a masculine man beneath, and I asked one of them out on a date. It didn't work very well, and most of the time they just whispered about me in the bathroom. It was an awkward age to be a boy, an age when girls were angels to me—never sinning, never breathing, and never going to the bathroom. They lived in heaven, pillow fighting in their pajamas while I was stuck on earth, struggling with puberty.

High school could not have come sooner. My hormones took an Alka-Seltzer, my sense of humor, a steroid, and my fast, red Acura landed me more dates than I had weekends to enjoy them. Oh, I had read *I Kissed Dating Goodbye*, and Joshua Harris's arguments were admirable, but never did I have the guts to go through with them. The only things I kissed good-bye were the girls I took to dinner. I was a dating machine, or so I thought. The local florist knew my name, I stocked up on Tic Tacs, and I could have bought another red car with all the money I spent on movies, candy, and popcorn. Dating was the drug of choice, and I wrote myself a new prescription every week.

RUSSIAN REDEMPTION

But Nadia was a pill I could not pop.

"No," I told her. "I can't have sex with you."

She burst into tears and ran back to her cabin, embarrassed, abandoned, and shocked. She had offered herself to me, and I had rejected her—the Russian cookie had crumbled, and I spent most of the night praying for her and praising God for helping me make that decision.

The next morning was an awkward one. I found Nadia eating breakfast, and she avoided me at first. But over the next few days, we became genuine friends. We continued talking about the Christian faith, and I told her about how it had changed my life. Several days later, she told me that I was the only man who had ever said no to her for sex, and before our team left for America, I gave her my Bible.

Leaving the Russian camp was one of the hardest things I've ever had to do. The orphans had attached themselves to us. They viewed us as friends and caretakers who, like their parents, were now abandoning them. I wanted to adopt every one of them and bring them back to America. Theirs would be the finest health care available, the best school systems around, and the freedom to worship Christ in a church where everyone knew their names. Theirs would have been heaven, but I had to leave them in hell. And to this day I can still feel their arms, grabbing and clawing at me to stay as I boarded the bus.

I brooded the whole way to the airport. I thought about my upbringing, being born in America with two amazing parents, a sister, and an ugly but cheerful dog named Snowball. I didn't deserve those things. I didn't deserve the Christmas presents and the birthday cakes. I didn't deserve the pleasant childhood memories. I was never abandoned, and my sister wasn't trafficked for sex. And I couldn't help but pray for Nadia and the orphans in Russia as our plane taxied to the runway.

SATAN'S PROSTITUTES

God created us in His image to be His mirror. When He looked down at us, He saw Himself. He saw the creativity, the ability to communicate, the immortality, and the intimacy. But after Adam and Eve sinned, the mirror cracked. No longer were we perfect representations of God. We were shattered glass, broken bottles, flawed and fractured mirrors that distorted God's holy face. We exchanged our first love for another, and with legs wide open we prostituted ourselves to the serpent. We pimped our passions to the Devil like unholy whores. Beauty became the beast, and we could not even look at God. Moses tried, but his face burned so brightly that he had to wear a sack over his head to protect the people from the rays (see Exodus 34:35). When once we walked in the cool of the garden, our sin led us into the wilderness, and we wandered around, looking for another Eden.

God in His grace, however, didn't let us wander by ourselves. He came down to our level in the person of Jesus Christ and restored communion with creation. The apostle Paul tells us that "God put the wrong on him who never did anything wrong, so we could be put right with God" (2 Corinthians 5:21). In other words, God beat His little boy with the belt reserved for us, and we agree with Isaiah: "Through his bruises we get healed" (Isaiah 53:5). On the roller coaster of redemption, Jesus Christ sank from the heights of heaven to the very depths of hell.

But hell was not the ending. On the third day, He arose from the dead, ascended into heaven, and now reigns as King with His Father. Through intimacy with Jesus Christ the mirror is restored, and when God looks down at us He does not see shattered souls deserving punishment but rather a polished image of His glory and grace.

∘ ∘ ∘ ∘ ∘ ∘

They say when you meet your soul mate everyone else in the world disappears. A crowd of two hundred becomes a crowd of two, and all that matters is the moment, the perfect moment when God has creation accomplish His will. For three wonderful years Rebecca and I became best friends. We talked until the wee hours of the morning, ate most of our meals together, and drove around the city just for driving's sake. Because we didn't want to jeopardize our relationship, we limited our physical attention. We drafted an "Ode to the Sustaining of Friendship in a Relationship."[1] It was a puppy dog love with an electric fence around it, and our friendship survived the years.

Rebecca and I grew together spiritually too. The days of high school were in the past. No more selfish dating and "living-for-the-moment" mentalities. The fast, red Acura rarely broke the speed limit, and I began to love Rebecca's love for the Lord. I also started reading my Bible in the mornings and digging through those Old Testament books that nobody preaches on anymore, like Nahum and Obadiah. During church, Rebecca and I wrote notes to each other. Her questions about God enthused me to know more, read more, and learn more, and though I didn't always have the right answer, our quest for spiritual enlightenment brought us together.

I told her about my adventures and pilgrimages around the world—adventures through Europe, Great Britain, Asia, and Russia. I told her stories about mossy castles and foreign foods. I told her about my cravings for sushi and my passion for writing. We shared deep secrets—secrets that I had never told anyone before. But there was one secret I kept to myself. It was a secret too sacred to say, even to Rebecca, my best friend. At night, I took my secret from its case and admired its sparkly edges. They say "secrets" like these last forever, and I had emptied my savings account to afford it.

In many ways, falling in love with Christ was like falling in love with Rebecca. The more time I spent with God, the more I loved Him. God gives us the desire for intimacy so He can satisfy it. We often sing the words, "Come, Thou Fount of every blessing, tune my heart to sing Thy grace,"[2] but so often our hearts are tuned to every frequency but the Father's. We listen to secularism but avoid the God who calls us to be pilgrims in this land. We listen to materialism but ignore the One who owns the cattle on a thousand hills. Only when we tune to God by prayer, worship, and intimate studying of the Scripture can we finish the hymn, "Let Thy grace, Lord, like a fetter, bind my wandering heart to Thee."[3]

> God gives us the desire for intimacy so He can satisfy it.

The Bible is the greatest love story ever told—a divine valentine licked, sealed, and stamped by the power of the Holy Spirit, and it speaks with great clarity to us today. "'I have loved you,' says the LORD" (Malachi 1:2 NIV). What kind of love is this? It is a former love, a past-tense love, a love that saw every sin, every lie. A love that Teresa of Ávila understood when she wrote that God's love for us is like two wax candles joining "to such an extent that the flame coming from them is one."[4] The love of God is a former love, melting us to Him—but it is also a frequent and a future love, continually disciplining and washing us in the light of His glory.

o o o o o o

I became a man at a Barnes & Noble at 9:45 p.m. Up until that day, life was a playground, and I was at recess. But as I looked Rebecca's father in the eye to ask him for his daughter's hand in marriage, I discovered a new definition of manhood. "I love your daughter more than anything in the world," I told him. "And I want to spend the rest of my life making her happy."

What an odd tradition—a strange boy asking a father for the life of his little girl. How counterintuitive it must have been for him to say, "Welcome to the family." He raised her, loved her, disciplined her, and prayed for her. He was there when she learned how to walk and talk, when she learned to ride a bicycle and drive a car. When she was happy, he laughed with her. When she was sad, he cried with her. Such was the relationship between this father and his daughter, and there I was, a semi-polished stranger, asking him if I could take her away. Had it been me, on the other side of the table, I would have said no. I would have said, "Hey kid, crawl back into the hole where you came from, and while you're there get a haircut." But he gave me his blessing, he gave me a hug, and then he gave me his precious little girl.

> # Christians are God's boomerangs. . . . He bends us back to Himself.

I asked Rebecca to marry me on a Friday. The lights were low and the breeze was cool. I took her to a fountain where we had both thrown pennies into the water, wishing that one day we would be married. My hands were shaking and my knees were knocking as I looked her in the eyes, but the timing had never been better. Romance was in the air, and I dropped to my knee and asked her to be my wife.

We may never fully know why God bends down from heaven to engage our hearts. It's not because He needed us. Before we were screaming in our cribs, God was complete in Himself. Saint Augustine said that God was satisfied in Himself because of the love each member of the Trinity shared for the other, but we praise Him for being vulnerable with us and saving us from our sins.

It is a mystery—the synergism of salvation. Jesus once said, "The Father who sent me is in charge. He draws people to me—that's the only way you'll ever come" (John 6:44). Yet, He also said, "By believing in him, anyone can have a whole and lasting life" (John 3:16). We will never perfectly connect these two truths, but we must believe that they work together. We will never know where our swimming starts and God's reeling ends, but we do know one thing: When divinity desires humanity, a beautiful chemistry follows.

Christians are God's boomerangs. He formed us in the womb, throws us in the world, and bends us back to Himself. Since our pilgrimages start and end with God, He becomes the apple of our eyes. He is the center of our thoughts, deeds, music, and worship. When we fall in love with God, sin no longer satisfies us. Our fleshly passions are exchanged for a new temptation, a fresh temptation, a temptation for holiness. We are given taste buds for a different kind of food—a heavenly kind. And we are no longer satisfied with kissing our Creator with the veil between our mouths.

○ ○ ○ ○ ○ ○

The wedding cake sat alone on the reception table. The halls were hollow and the pews were empty. Soon, nearly four hundred people would show up for the ceremony. Pictures would be taken and hands would be shaken, but for the moment I was in the dressing room looking in the mirror. John spoke of the church as being the bride of Christ (Revelation 19:7), and I couldn't wait to see my very own. My best man, David Riker, offered some well-intentioned sex tips as the pastor walked into the room. But all the awkwardness was forgotten when beauty took the form of a bride and walked down the aisle.

I stood at the front of the sanctuary and watched her. Shakespeare would have been speechless. Her beauty was breathtaking and stunning. As Rebecca's eyes met mine, I knew I was looking in the mirror; she was my other half and man, did I want to be whole! For the first time in my life I was ready to say 'yes.' Yes to happiness. Yes to hardships. Yes to smiles and yes to trials. Yes to sex, marriage, and intimacy. And the kiss, well . . . let's just say it was a long time coming.

Plastic surgeons are always making mountains out of molehills.

—DOLLY PARTON

naked
with God

SO I'M TYPING in Starbucks, sipping a semi-warm, extra-whipped cream venti chai latté. It's not ideal for writing—the noise, traffic, and hustle and bustle. But there's nothing like a strong dose of caffeine to get the brain in gear. People of all types step in. There's the doctor getting ready for a long day, the soccer mom treating herself to a five-minute espresso, and of course the frantic college student who stayed up all night cramming for an exam.

Suddenly, a cell phone rings. It's an ordinary ring, the kind that comes with the phone. Everyone stops what they're doing to check. It rings again. *Somebody gonna get that?* Purses are scrambled through, pockets emptied. Again it rings. *How many rings does it take, people?* Suddenly I realize where the ring is coming from. Reaching down into my laptop case, I pull my cell phone to my ear and take the call with a shade of embarrassment in my voice.

I have a sweet setup. In my leather laptop case are my MacBook Pro, BibleWorks electronic Bible, wireless Internet digital voice recorder, iPod, and a digital camera. OK, a confession: I am hungry for hardware, starving for software, and completely intoxicated with upgrading. Maybe it's my high-tech generation. Maybe it's the media's fault for whetting my appetite with gadgets and gigabytes. Perhaps it's a power issue. The more stuff I own, the more control I have over life. The better the GPS device, the calmer I feel in the middle of an interstate highway. Whatever the reason, the result is undeniable—I am digitizing myself to death.

Recently I took a pilgrimage to Italy. My father and I wanted to retrace the steps of Saint Francis of Assisi, and while most of my friends were partying at the beach for spring break, I sat in the Atlanta airport, eager to board the plane. Above me, a forty-two-inch flat-screen plasma TV aired a CNN presentation on the war in Iraq, but I was too consumed by the sophisticated businessmen beside me. One of them was uptight, arguing on his sleek space-age cell phone about how he was going to fire an employee upon his return. Two others exchanged eye-rolling glances as they typed on their handheld PDAs (those personal digital assistants that keep all of life's appointments, contacts, and plans at your fingertips). Their fingers were comically large for the keys, but they seemed to take pride in their new gadgets. And who could blame them? In the palm of their hands they held the entire Internet. A world of knowledge was at their command. Had Alexander the Great, Napoleon, or even Adolf Hitler possessed such information, the world could have turned out very differently.

Eventually we landed in Rome, a truly worthy destination for a pilgrimage. Not only is the city filled with ancient churches and sacred spaces, but there's practically a history lesson around every corner. Founded in the eighth century before Christ, Rome quickly became a bastion for technology. The newly invented concrete allowed Romans to construct unprecedented structures such as the Pantheon, the largest unreinforced concrete dome in the history of the world. Militarily, crossbows and catapults aided the Roman army as they conquered the known world, and aqueducts supplied water throughout their world. In Rome itself were more than two hundred sixty miles of aqueducts. Historians say that they even used the aqueducts to fill up the Coliseum with water for naval battles.

We had only three days in Rome, and I didn't want to leave without seeing the burial site of the apostle Paul and the Church of the Immaculate Conception whose crypt is decorated with skulls and bones. On Sunday, we went to an Anglican worship service, saw the tomb of Monica, the mother of Saint Augustine, and viewed the burial site of Justin Martyr, an early Christian apologist.

THE PILGRIM AND LADY POVERTY

In 1206, another young man, named Francis, took a pilgrimage to Rome. He was in his twenties and searching for God in radical ways. Rome attracted tens of thousands of pilgrims because of its legend that Saint Peter was buried just outside its walls. In a spirit of inquiry, Francis traveled the one hundred miles from his home in Assisi to see it. As he approached the sanctuary that Constantine erected in 330, he pushed through peasants and beggars to get a glimpse of Saint Peter's tomb. To his disgust, he saw poor peasants throwing the few coins they had through the grate. Francis, too, took a handful of coins and chunked them as hard as he could against it, no doubt raising some eyebrows. Little did he know that within thirty years, a similar basilica would be constructed in his honor at Assisi.

In his youth, Francis wanted to be a warrior. Entranced by the Knights of the Round Table, Francis purchased armor and enlisted in the army. Since his family was wealthy, he would have ridden out to battle in the cavalry division. Unfortunately, his dreams were shattered when his friends were slaughtered at Perugia and he was taken into captivity. After a year in prison, he fell sick and his father bought his freedom, only for Francis to squander it with wild living and expensive parties back home.

One day at a drinking party, his friends noticed that Francis seemed bored with his life of debauchery. The wine held no more magic for him, and the games were growing dull. "Are you ever going to get married?" they asked him, laughingly.

Francis was not laughing. For quite some time, his dreams and nightmares were pulling him away from his old habits. His heart felt strangely warm as the world grew strangely dim. "Oh yes," he replied. "I will marry a fairer bride than any of you have ever seen."

"And who will that be, Francis?"

"Lady Poverty," he said with a grin on his face.

After Francis returned from his pilgrimage to Rome, he went back to Assisi and began begging. One day, while praying at the Church of San Damiano, he was sure he heard Jesus speaking through a wooden cross, telling him to rebuild His church. This was a turning point in the life of Francis, and with great fervor he abandoned his passions for partying and began his ministry.

His father, a wealthy merchant, didn't approve of his son's new lifestyle. Why would a son give up a life of health and wealth? Why would he give his expensive clothes away? It didn't make sense. In a desperate attempt to change Francis's mind, his father held a court to cast judgment on his son and hold him accountable for all the money he had borrowed to give to the poor. Naturally, the town was buzzing with gossip about this family quarrel, and many showed up for the showdown.

The morning of the trial, Francis dressed well for once. The bishop, who presided over the court, said, "Your father is very angry with you and deeply offended. You tell me you wish to be religious. Well, then, you must give him back the money you have taken, since you may not have legally acquired it."[1]

DROPPING MATERIALISM . . . AND CLOTHES

All eyes were on Francis to see his reaction. Would he return the money and appease his father? Would he keep the money and be disowned by his family? With firm resolution, Francis stood to his feet and said, "Not the money only, my lord, for that belongs to him. All my clothes also."[2] In front of everyone, Francis took off his robe and let it fall to his feet. A unified gasp circled the scene as naked Francis bent over to present both his robe and the money bag to the bishop. Mothers and fathers covered the eyes of their daughters, but Lady Poverty looked on with great admiration. Francis had finally abandoned himself to God, and there was no turning back. He was willing to get naked with God.

> I dreamed of driving cars so fast that my face would peel from its bones. I wanted it all.

After leaving Rome, I traveled to Assisi to stand in the place where Francis shed his quest for materialism. Today, it's called the Piazza of Santa Maria Maggiore. With a backpack hanging from my shoulders, I tried to imagine what Francis felt. I tried to understand what Jesus said to the rich young man: "There's one thing left: Go sell whatever you own and give it to the poor. All your wealth will then be heavenly wealth" (Mark 10:21). Was I willing to let go of my worldly longings? Was I capable of cutting loose my lust for hard drives, superior browsing capabilities, and recently released PlayStation games?

Not a chance. Green hybrid cars passed by the square, taking my heart and thoughts with them. So tight was my grip on gadgets that I fantasized about the hardware yet to be invented. I dreamed of driving cars so fast that my face would peel from its bones. I wanted it all—new shoes, new sunglasses, and new shaving cream warmers that provide fresh and exciting ways to trim my scruff. Nevertheless, since I was in a place known for stripping, I let the straps of my backpack slide down my shoulder. But since I had a rather pricey digital camera inside, it hit the ground gently and with great care. Plus, who wants to go to Assisi and pay a fine for public nudity?

Over the next five days we traveled through Umbria. Italians call it the green heart of Italy, and for good reason. Rolling hills laced with castles and orchids blurred by the window of our air-conditioned, manual transmission rental car. If Umbria really was a green heart, I enjoyed driving through its grassy arteries. We visited towns like Gubbio, where Francis tamed a wolf. We saw Spoleto and Orvieto, which Francis often visited. Each medieval village provoked a sense of conviction within me. I thought of Francis walking down their streets in rags, begging for money and depending on God for food.

From Assisi we drove a winding road up the side of Mount Subasio to see a place called the Carceri (Italian for "prison"), where Francis retreated to pray. It's a rugged environment, a place in the clouds that bears the brunt of nature's brutality. Even before Francis came here, the site was used as a jail to isolate criminals from the city life below. Although he had committed no crime, Francis placed himself in solitary confinement because he was still enslaved by his flesh. He felt chained to the habits of his former life. Though sincerely committed to Christ, Francis empathized with Paul who had the desire to do good, but couldn't carry it out (Romans 7:18-19). He often called himself Brother Ass and punished himself for straying from God. He put ashes on his food, plunged into snow, and even jumped on thorny briar patch bushes when tempted with sex.

With somewhat of a smirk on my face, I thought of Francis in the briar patch bush as we drove up to the Carceri. Where I come from, such a thing would be laughed at and then frowned upon. Nevertheless, if half of our ministers followed Francis's example in this area, we wouldn't have nearly the number of pastors addicted to pornography and other forms of sexual promiscuity (though the briar patches of the world might object).

It was spring in Italy as we continued to wind up the steep slopes. In the valley below Assisi, the rain had been pouring all morning. But as we ascended

> they are small caves chiseled by hands that were hungry to touch the face of God.

above the cloud line, sleet and snow accumulated on our windshield. Having packed for spring weather, my water-absorbent coat and shoes were not sufficient to fight off the biting blizzard. I was a pilgrim unprepared.

When we arrived at the summit, we were greeted by a view reserved only from hang gliders and small planes. We entered a tiny chapel that was cut into the side of the mountain and prayed for about fifteen minutes before exploring the surrounding woodlands. A path takes pilgrims around the side of the mountain from cave to cave where Francis and his monks prayed and lived. They are small caves, quaint caves, chiseled by hands that were hungry to touch the face of God. For days and weeks Francis wrestled with God in these holes, pouring out not only his life but also his health. He would later die an early death in his forties, but while alive, he wanted to serve God and court Lady Poverty. He spent weeks with her, wooing her attention and winning her affection. He once prayed:

Lord, show me Poverty
whom you loved so dearly.
Merciful Jesus,
have pity on me:
I am full of yearning
for my Lady Poverty;
I can find no peace without her.
You, Lord, it was who first
aroused love for her in my heart;
grant me the privilege
of possessing her. . . .
Jesus, you were very poor,
and I want to call
nothing under heaven mine
but only to live
on what others may give me.[3]

As I stooped to enter the cave of Brother Leone, my bladder reminded me of its presence. *Not now. Not in such a sacred spot!* Nature was calling, and it was not going to leave a message. Since I was in the forest without a restroom, I turned around to make sure no one was looking, and then relieved myself near the prayer cave. I felt terrible about it. What disrespect for the monks who worshiped here!

But then I remembered that these monks would have done the same thing. They would have emptied not only their bladders, but also their bowels. The forest was their home. It was their family room, prayer closet, and bathroom. These were radical men with raw faith. They were Jesus freaks who detached themselves from pride and wealth to live a life of adoration for the Savior.

I zipped up my pants before the blizzard permanently damaged my manhood, and I realized that I had emptied more than just my bladder. During those twenty awkward seconds, I had participated in the same act as all the monks who peed and prayed here. This was the essence of the monastic way of life—a life of austerity, devotion, survival, and sacred intercourse with God. Standing there in the snow, I felt my passion for technology and materialism flowing out of me.

And with the eyes of a child, I looked around. There were no telephone poles, streetlights, or coffee shacks. There were no jazz clubs, sushi bars, or Internet cafés. It was pure nature, the way God created it. How can a forty-two-inch plasma television compare to what God has made? Can it capture a sunset or reproduce a forest breeze? Can it splash you with water or cool you with shade? No, at best it can only reproduce it at two-dimensional 1080p. It was the difference between drinking chlorinated city water and natural spring water. As I surveyed the trees, the earth, and the snow, I felt attracted to them. There was something magnetizing about the simple life, the rustic life, the life completely in love with the Lover. And I walked back to the trail a bit lighter than before.

KOBAYASHI CHRISTIANITY

Takeru Kobayashi has become a household name for those who watch competitive speed-eating contests. Born in 1978, Kobayashi rose to fame when he broke previous records for hot-dog-eating competitions throughout the world. In 2006 he ate over fifty-three hot dogs in twelve minutes for the new world record.[4] He is also the reigning champion of the Krystal Square Off World Hamburger Eating Championship and the Glutton Bowl, and he won the Alka-Seltzer US Open of Competitive Eating in 2005. Before competing, Kobayashi expands his stomach by eating large amounts of food. Every day he consumes an average of six thousand calories, exercises to burn away excess weight, and maintains 6 percent body fat. He is aided by gastroptosis, a displacement of his stomach that allows it to expand below the rib cage.

I've never won a food eating competition, unless we count that time I got my picture on the wall of Cheeburger Cheeburger for eating over a pound of hamburger. But I have put away some serious Southern cooking in my time. You can't be raised in the deep South without consuming slabs of barbecue, yams, okra, and fried chicken. These were the foods of my youth—creamed corn, mashed potatoes, and pecan pie—foods that stretch the pants of the Bible belt. My Sundays were made of sermons and cornbread, washed down with a little buttermilk. The women in our church labored for hours in the kitchen, making homemade casseroles and fried green tomatoes.

every day Francis gorged himself on God.

Kobayashi has much to teach me about Christianity. What would happen if I took in as much spiritual food as Kobayashi takes in physical food? Would I pop? How large is my spiritual stomach? Do I daily expand it? Do I even crave a bigger reservoir of faithfulness? Is it a sin to be a spiritual glutton? What would happen if I gave as much time to the Bible as I do to whatever happens to be on my car radio?

Francis force-fed himself with the things of God. He craved the Christ who loved him. Jesus did not load His cross into the back of a silver Saab and drive it to His death. He didn't buy expensive houses with pools and palm trees. He never chilled with His disciples in the lap of Israeli luxury. He was a poor peasant who had no home to brag about. He once told His disciples, "Are you ready to rough it? We're not staying in the best inns, you know" (Matthew 8:20).

Francis found a freedom in this way of life. He found comfort in total dependency on God. There was no mortgage for him to pay, no insurance to worry about. If he was hungry, God sent food. If he was lonely, God sent friends. Though he was scantly clad, Francis was wrapped in righteousness. The Holy Spirit oozed from him, and people knew he had been with Jesus. Every day Francis gorged himself on God, and his soul was only satisfied with the Christ who required ultimate sacrifice.

Near the end of his life, Francis was traveling through Egypt during a crusade. In his youth, he would have sacrificed greatly to fight in one of these armies. What a dream it would have been to re-

> poverty stared us in the face. I almost saw Francis among them, hands outstretched.

claim Jerusalem from the hands of the Muslims. But instead of bringing a sword of death, Francis offered the gift of eternal life. And the Egyptian sultan was so impressed with the humility of Francis that he allowed the monk safe passage back to Assisi.

Francis speaks loudly to our evangelical tradition. Make no mistake about it, I'm a born-and-bred, dyed-in-the-wool, happy and healthy Southern Baptist who holds his tradition with pride and pleasure. And as such, I do not always see eye to eye on every theological point held by my Catholic friends. But having been to Assisi, I recognize that Saint Francis can teach me about my faith. Francis had a missionary mind-set and a passion for personal conversion that foreshadowed my own denomination's zeal for carrying the gospel to the ends of the earth, and he challenges me to reconsider my devotion to Jesus Christ. He reminds my knees to become better acquainted with the ground they are made of. At times, he even says, "Christian, where is your humility, gentleness, and lowliness? Are you hungry for God, or are you full of yourself? What are your spiritual disciplines?

Why aren't you praying, fasting, and listening to God like you promised? Do you even weep for the world?"

In Rome, I remember seeing a paraplegic man sitting on a skateboard by the Trevi Fountain. He was begging for money. Tourists like me passed by, trying not to look, trying to enjoy the beauty of Lorenzo Bernini's architectural masterpiece. We had come to see water flowing over rocks and stony creatures. We had come to see the famous god, Neptune, taming the waters and his Tritons wrestling sea horses into submission. Those were the things we wanted to see as we tossed three coins into the fountain, as the tradition goes, hoping one day to return to the Eternal City.

But the poor begged for our attention. Against the backdrop of the splashy scenery, poverty stared us in the face. I almost saw Francis among them, hands outstretched, asking us to give him his daily bread. And for the first time in my life, I could not look away. His eyes were wide and gentle, and within them I did not see an Italian stranger on a skateboard; I saw Christ on a cross. I saw the Lord who called me to clothe the naked and feed the poor. I saw the One who left His riches in heaven to sink to earth and hell. And the strange part about it—he saw me too. He saw an American tourist, perhaps even a Christian, walking right by on legs that were strong and dependable. He saw a pair of eyes, perhaps the first of the day that were glued to his. And I emptied not only my pockets for the paraplegic beggar, but also my soul.

Francis could have been a wealthy man. He probably would have become a successful merchant, lawyer, or doctor. He could have experienced a long and healthy life, with women, riches, and glory hanging from every limb. But history erases those kinds of people. We remember Francis because he stripped his life of all that hindered his calling. We remember him because he didn't want to be remembered; he sought to decrease instead of increase in this world. Instead of vanity, Francis embodied humility. He shows us a life of obedience and purpose, a life of service to Him who assures us that Christians will taste the thorns before we touch the rose.

○ ○ ○ ○ ○ ○

I still write at Starbucks. How can I avoid it with the smell of gourmet coffee brewing in the background? But with each cup that is emptied, I remember the time in Assisi when I stood in the snow, peeing away my passion for technology. And with each sentence I write, I am reminded of Saint Francis, who worshiped the Savior with prayers like this:

> Most high, glorious God,
> enlighten the darkness of my heart
> and give me, Lord,
> a correct faith,
> a perfect charity,
> sense and knowledge,
> so that I may carry out your holy and true command.[5]

I'm no theologian. I don't know who or what God is.
All I know is He's more powerful than mom and dad put together.

—LISA SIMPSON

who's
your daddy?

MY DAD can beat up your dad."

I laughed. "In your dreams."

"He played football in college," Alex said, "and he can put your dad on the ground!"

"Doubt it."

"Bring it on," he said, throwing a basketball at my head. With a hollow *THUD*, the basketball bounced off my face. Everything went from red to black.

Awaking to a bloody nose and a terrible headache, I tried to stand up but was too dizzy. I hated bullies. Maybe it was their size, or their arrogance, or quite possibly their ability to get away with everything. Whatever the reason, I hated them with every ounce of my third-grade soul. Granted, I was skinny as a rail, forced to wear suspenders to keep my pants up, but this toothpick was sick of collecting trash from

Alex's mouth, and deep down I wanted my dad to rearrange his face.

Many years ago, on Mount Carmel in the northern part of Israel, a showdown took place between gods. The prophet Elijah called for a contest to see which god was the greatest. Elijah ordered two bulls to be slaughtered, one for Baal and the other for the God of Israel. The first god to send fire down from heaven would be worshiped as the winner. Four hundred and fifty prophets of Baal stepped up to the challenge. In those days, Baal was worshiped under many names, mainly as the sun god who rode on thunderclouds, forking fire through the sky. He was also referred to as "Lord of the Flies" (2 Kings 1:2).[1] Yet, no matter what name they used, Baal's bull remained raw, cold, and dripping with blood.

"What's wrong?" Elijah asked, taunting them. "Is Baal going to the bathroom?"

The evil prophets prayed harder.

"Maybe the Lord of the Flies is stuck in the ointment."

They danced around the altar, cutting themselves and shouting. (You can read Elijah's chiding words and the false prophets' responses in 1 Kings 18:27–28.)

"Has the god of lightning blown a fuse?" Elijah mused.[2]

After almost a day of this, Elijah approached the altar. It was his turn. He repaired the stones that the Baalites desecrated, dug a trench around the bull, and doused the whole thing three times in water. Elijah wanted them to know that it was God who would cause the fire, not two rocks rubbing together.

Stepping towards the altar, Elijah prayed, "O God, God of Abraham, Isaac, and Israel, make it known right now that you are God in Israel" (1 Kings 18:36). And suddenly, holy heat fell from heaven—fire hot enough to barbeque the bull, consume the stones, and lick up the water from the trench. Then Elijah had the people who witnessed

God's power seize the prophets of Baal and slaughter them in the Valley of Kishon.

Until I read this story, I thought that God was a geek, a pathetic force who liked ice cream and marshmallows. When I first heard in Sunday school that Jesus was knocking on the door of my heart, I felt sorry for Him all alone out there. "Somebody let Him in," I thought. "Look at Jesus, all freezing and shaking like that! Poor guy. It must be five degrees below zero, not to mention the wind chill. For crying out loud, give Him a towel, some dry underwear, and a warm cup of hot chocolate. For God's sake, somebody let Jesus into your heart!"

But the more I studied the Scriptures, the more I realized that my interpretation of God had been all wrong. Jesus doesn't stand at the door and knock for *His* sake, but for *ours*. Our hearts are on fire. Sin has so inflamed us, corrupted and consumed us, that were it not for our Father the firefighter, we would burn to death in our rebellion against Him.

> when God flexes His muscles, the heavens are rearranged. He curls constellations with His biceps.

The apostle Paul was so ablaze when God met him on the road to Damascus that Christ had to kick in the dead bolt of his heart, knock him to the ground, and roll him around with the soothing of the Spirit. Paul needed some serious saving. He was the Osama bin Laden of the day, a religious terrorist. Yet, after he encountered Christ, he told the men of Athens, "The God who made the world and everything in it, this Master of sky and land, doesn't live in custom-made shrines or need the human race to run errands for him, as if he couldn't take care of himself" (Acts 17:25). God doesn't need defending any more than a velociraptor needs a fork and knife to cut its meat. "His powerful Word is sharp as a surgeon's scalpel, cutting through everything whether doubt or defense, laying us open to listen and obey" (Hebrews 4:12).

God is not a weak warrior. Just ask the Philistines who captured the ark of the covenant and placed it inside the temple of Dagon, their fertility god (1 Samuel 5). The next morning, Dagon had fallen in front of the ark. The Philistines picked him up, but the next day he fell again and his head and arms were chopped off. All that remained was a stump. God was not pleased with these pagan people, and He cursed them with tumors until they returned His ark to Israel. God has no competition. Ask the Assyrians who were about to attack Jerusalem. "I'll shield this city, I'll save this city," God told Judah's King Hezekiah (2 Kings 19:34), and an angel of the Lord slew 185,000 men.

Growing up, I did my best to work out in the gym. Only until I played varsity soccer in high school did I ever really put muscles on my frame, but even that wasn't so spectacular. When I flex my arm, not much happens, but when God flexes His muscles, the heavens are rearranged. He curls constellations with His biceps, swirls galaxies with His triceps, and throws Saturns like Frisbees across this universe. The cosmos is His playground, a celestial sandbox, and when He said, "Let there be light" (Genesis 1:3 NIV), darkness scatted like a frightened cat.

I had to exchange the buddy Jesus I knew for the exalted Christ who lowered Himself to my level that I might be rescued from the destruction of death. Only then was I able to worship God in spirit and in truth (see John 4:23). When we get a true glimpse of God, our faith takes flight. When we see the Creator "sitting on a throne—high, exalted!—and the train of his robes filled the Temple" (Isaiah 6:1), church gains meaning for our lives. Hymns encourage us and sermons nourish us. When we confess with the psalmist that "God's glory is on tour in the skies, God-craft on exhibit across the horizon" (Psalm

19:1), we approach the presence of God knowing that the One who washed His disciples' feet sits on a throne that spans the skies. King David saw God in this way. In Psalm 18:13-16, he wrote:

> Then God thundered out of heaven; the High God gave a great shout, spraying hailstones and fireballs. God shoots His arrows—pandemonium! He hurls His lightnings—a rout! The secret sources of ocean are exposed, the hidden depths of earth lie uncovered. . . . But me He caught—reached all the way from sky to sea; He pulled me out of that ocean of hate, that enemy chaos, the void in which I was drowning.

God is always bending down to us. On every page of the Bible His posture is portrayed. He bent down to deliver David from enemies, Daniel from lions, and Jonah from drowning. And one starry night in the little town of Bethlehem, God bent way down. He bent down so far that He became a man. And He reached down to heal lepers and lift up prostitutes. He reached down to save Peter from his sinking situation. And when we feel that all is evil and wrong, when hell and death wrap their arms around us, God reaches down and reminds us that we are glued to His holy hand. We are concreted to the Christ who gives us the power of the Holy Spirit. And we become the fire through which God ignites the world.

ON GOD AND GREECE

During the apostle Paul's second missionary journey, he visited Greece (Acts 17). It was not a pleasant experience for him, and he left the city with only a handful of converts. Paul must have felt so out of place in Athens, an educated Jew surrounded by thousands of pagan gods and idols. With such an array of deities, the Athenians wanted to be sure they didn't leave any god out of their worship, so they created a statue to the "unknown god."

As Paul was walking through the marketplace, he noticed this statue. Being a tent maker, Paul was a master of weaving, and he threaded the gospel of God around this idol. He told the stoic and epicurean philosophers about the one true God who reigns eternally. They listened to Paul, though they probably didn't recognize the name of Jesus Christ. To them, it sounded like their Ionic goddess of health. But Paul's Jesus was different. He was a divine being who was born of flesh and blood. He was God and man. The Athenians loved to hear these new ideas, and they dragged Paul up to the Aereopagus, called Mars Hill by the Romans, a large rock at the foot of the Acropolis, so he could share his testimony.

> the Bible is the breath of God, vapors of fuel set on fire by the Holy Spirit.

With a Bible in my hand, I stood in the same spot where Paul preached. The stones beneath my feet had been smoothed by millions of people throughout history. It could have been a rock from Mars itself, jagged yet curvy, foreign to the surrounding landscape. My wife and I had come to Athens for pilgrimage purposes, and also for hard-core, inner-city ministry.

I scanned the mountains on the horizon and thought about Paul who incorporated Greek poets and philosophers like the Cretan poet Epimenides and Aratus the Cilician into his speech.[3] The Parthenon stood behind us, a mathematically perfect building dedicated to the goddess Athena. Paul must have turned around to see it too. The Parthenon once had been the pride of Greece, but now, in the twenty-first century, it was temporarily surrounded with scaffolding, like teeth covered in braces. With pagan temples bleaching in the sun behind us, I now held the Word of God in my hands. Unlike man-made structures, the Bible had survived the ages intact.

What is the Bible, anyway? For King David the Bible was a breath of fresh air, for "the revelation of God is whole and pulls our lives together" (Psalm 19:7). And for Paul, too, "every part of Scripture is God-breathed" (2 Timothy 3:16). Jesus used Scripture as a weapon against Satan. When He was tempted in the wilderness, He attacked the Devil with the words, "It is written . . ." (Matthew 4:4 NIV). The Bible is the breath of God, vapors of fuel set on fire by the Holy Spirit. And when we encounter the Bible, we discover that it has already encountered us. Day by day, we discover that the God who sends fire down from heaven has sent heaven down by the fire of His holy Word. Through it we encounter the living God.

○ ○ ○ ○ ○ ○

My in-laws gave me a remote-controlled airplane for my birthday several years ago. Flight has always interested me, and I love studying the flight sketches of Leonardo da Vinci. This was my kind of present. After charging the battery for the craft's maiden flight, I strapped the wing to the top of my AeroBird Extreme and threw it into the air. It was a miniature leap of faith, a tiny act of trust, and I held my breath as the screaming propellers pulled the plane into the air.

And then it crashed.

How could this happen? What had I done wrong? Several weeks later, I launched it again into the sky. This time it was going to be different. Having bought a new wing, I felt confident that the wind would welcome my plane into its proximity.

It didn't. In fact, the crash was almost impressive. Going to the store a third time for parts was embarrassing. But Wilbur and Orville Wright didn't give up, and neither would I. After several weeks of training on a computer flight simulator, I grew comfortable with the principles of flight. Launching it into the air the third time, I found the plane easier to fly. It was a hot afternoon and the sun was blinding, but I soared that plane at full throttle, soaking up the confidence that comes from defying gravity.

Suddenly, I noticed that my plane was not alone in the air. A giant brown and tan hawk circled above it. Even though the Aero-Bird Extreme had a four-foot wingspan, this hawk began to investigate it, and I assumed its nest was in the area. To my shock, the hawk attacked my plane. For three exciting minutes, the hawk and I had something of a dogfight (or a birdfight) a hundred feet off the ground. I swooped, it swooped; I dove, it dove. And just when the battle was getting good, the battery of my plane died and my plane fell to the earth and crashed again.

As I loaded the broken pieces of my plane in the car, the hawk continued to fly above, circling us with a smile on its beak. I would have been smiling too—if I had a paintball gun in my hand. But instead, I drove away thinking about how man's creation cannot compare to God's creation. The plastic of my plane could not compare to the blood and bones of that bird.

○ ○ ○ ○ ○ ○

Standing on Mars Hill, I read Acts 17, thinking of what Paul would say if only he could see the pagan buildings now, desecrated and crumbling. I could almost hear an "I told you so" on his lips. In his letter to Corinth, a city not far from Athens, he wrote, "So where can you find someone truly wise, truly educated, truly intelligent in this day and age? Hasn't God exposed it all as pretentious nonsense?" (1 Corinthians 1:20). It was a moment of great continuity for my faith, a moment when God's Word outlasted Greek temples. A few hundred years after Paul left Athens, the Parthenon became a Christian church, and nineteen centuries later, the national flag hanging beside the Parthenon would be lowered to half-staff on Good Friday and raised on Easter morning in recognition of Christ's resurrection.

The pagan beliefs had not prevailed, and God had triumphed where Paul had failed. Standing there, I felt proud to have a Father who is in heaven. Jesus said, "Sky and earth will wear out; my words won't wear out" (Matthew 24:35).

But I am also glad to have a father who is on earth. Born in "hell's half acre" in Chattanooga, Tennessee, my father grew up in the ghetto. His mother suffered from polio, his father died in prison, and they never had enough food to eat. Yet despite these circumstances, the Lord sent a holy fire into the heart of young Timothy Francis George. One night, eight-year-old Timothy gave his life to Christ. He gave it all to God—his mind, his will, and his future. And God gave him lots too. He gave him the ability to learn, speak, and study. He began preaching revivals across Tennessee and the southeastern states. He went to Harvard, became a seminary professor in Kentucky, and eventually founded Beeson Divinity School in Birmingham, Alabama. (He now is considered by many to be one of the leading historical theologians in American evangelicalism.)

> is God susceptible to defeat? Satan thought so. . . . But on the third day, Jesus Christ was raised to life and the Devil was laid to rest.

He's a world-class scholar, but he's also a great dad. When I was young, he taught me to play racquetball. Now, racquetball is a game of angles, speed, and strategy. Being a young boy, I walked onto the court, small and wiry, half the size of my dad. And no matter how many times I swung at the ball, young David could not defeat Goliath. With great patience, he served the ball. I swung and missed, swung and missed—hundreds of times—swinging and missing, falling down and standing up. Then one day, perhaps by sheer coincidence, I actually hit the ball back. It shocked the pants off my dad, and the ball hit him on the thigh, causing a welt that would ripen into a juicy, purple bruise.

The older I grew, the harder he served the ball. What once was soft now was slammed, and I continued to swing and miss, swing and miss. The game got faster, the shots trickier, but for a while he had me believing I was actually progressing in my skill. Little did I know that all he had to do was turn up the heat and I would be left in the dust. These days, his arthritis has shown favor on me, and I pay him back for all those embarrassing years of ball whiffing. But every once in a while, I'll see a twinkle in his eye, and he'll reduce me to a five-year-old boy swinging a racket that was as big as I was.

It's good to have a Father who controls the game. I remember seeing a painting in a European museum where God was playing the Devil at a game of chess. God was apparently losing; the Devil had a huge smile on his skeleton face, and the title of the painting was *Checkmate*. I stood there, puzzled by the picture. Could it be true? Is God susceptible to defeat?

Satan thought so. Pilate had Jesus beaten, flogged, and tortured. In the ultimate game of chess, it looked as if God were losing. Yet God was executing His righteous judgment on sin. As Christ embraced the nails, the crown of thorns, and the crucifixion, God bent down—this time with a whip of wrath. No dove descended that day when the Father crushed His Son for our sins. In fact, hell was on holiday. But what the Devil didn't know, what Satan couldn't see, was that God had one more move. And on the third day, Jesus Christ was raised to life and the Devil was laid to rest, and with His holy hand God used His one more move to prove His all-time love.

That is why we can sing with Martin Luther, "The prince of darkness grim, we tremble not for him; his rage we can endure, for lo, his doom is sure, one little word shall fell him."[4] The monster we fight is a crippled creature. He is a vampire without fangs, a werewolf without claws, and a dragon without fire. We shouldn't flinch at him because Christ has crushed

> "you've abandoned everything for the sake of the gospel, yet you are richer than all the kings in the world."

the head of the serpent, as predicted in Genesis 3:15. While his body still slithers, the creature has a massive concussion and will one day be thrown into the lake of fire.

○ ○ ○ ○ ○ ○

Rebecca and I ministered to Persian refugees in Athens, Greece, who had fled their countries for political and economic reasons. These were young men and women who were trying to find better lives in better lands. Many had witnessed the murder of their family members under the Taliban regime; others had been persecuted and tortured for becoming Christians in a Muslim environment. Each refugee had a story, a history of grief and heartache. We spent many hours loving them, feeding and clothing them, and, in our spare time, playing grueling games of Ping-Pong with them. We were trying to be the hands and feet of Christ to those who needed gloves and shoes.

During a weekend retreat near Athens, I had the opportunity to speak to a group of refugees who had recently become Christians. They were young in their faith but zealous about their calling. When my translator, Mohsen, became a Christian in Iran, his wife divorced him. In fact, most of the refugees in the room had lost everything after becoming believers, and I felt unworthy to bring them a word about God. What had I ever sacrificed for my faith? What had Christ ever cost me? Maybe a couple of friends and some wild parties, but these were Christians who had paid a great price for their faith, and my knees knocked as I stood before them with the Word of God in my hands.

I looked at these faithful followers and began. "Maybe your hopes are gone, your homes are gone. Your dreams have died and your friends are gone. You've abandoned everything for the sake of the gospel, yet you are richer than all the kings in the world, for God has adopted you as sons and daughters of a heavenly home." I, a wealthy, sheltered American, looked into the eyes of those men and saw not a room of refugees, but a fellowship of kings. These were the real heroes of the faith, not me. And I hoped that their mansions in heaven (John 14:2) would be closer to God than mine.

God created us with the desire for adoption so He could be our Father. From the beginning of time, the blueprints of His love were sketched in His diary, and He accomplishes what has been forever arranged. The sin that orphaned us was laid on Christ, and through His death, burial, and resurrection we are issued passports into paradise. Yet even in paradise Jesus humbles Himself by sharing the spotlight with us. Paul writes, "Now if we are children, then we are heirs—heirs of God and co-heirs with Christ" (Romans 8:17 NIV). Since coheirs share the spoil, everything Christ owns we will own. Everything over which Christ rules we will rule. Everything Christ governs we will govern.

o o o o o o

Turns out, Alex didn't get in trouble for chunking that basketball in my face. The teachers were looking the other way and were occupied with other matters. In years to come, I would have many more days like these. But that's OK. Nothing on earth is hidden from God.

And He will judge this world, not with water again, but with fire. "But when the Day of God's Judgment does come, it will be unannounced, like a thief. The sky will collapse with a thunderous bang, everything disintegrating in a huge conflagration, earth and all its works exposed to the scrutiny of Judgment" (2 Peter 3:10). On that day, the divine thief will steal His saints away—away from bullies, bruises, and beatings. Away from sickness and suffering. And while the man-made structures of this earth crumble and melt, those who belong to God will be hurried to their heavenly home.

The eagle is a fascinating creature. It has a larger body, broader wings, and stronger talons than most birds of prey. Its eyesight is second to none in the animal kingdom, capable of seeing rabbits from two miles away. It's no wonder that some of the greatest empires in the history of civilization claimed the eagle as their national symbol— the Babylonians, the Roman Empire, and even the United States of America. Yet despite its strength and prowess, the eagle is not exempt from danger. When it feels threatened, the eagle does something no other bird can do—it flies directly into the sun, blinding its enemy. Scientists tell us that an eagle's eye has a special lens that allows it to look directly into the rays of the sun. Even in the first century, Pliny the Elder wrote that the eagle "forces its unfledged young to look at the rays of the sun; if any of them blinks or has watering eyes, those ones are thrown out of the nest."[5]

Christians are flying creatures too. According to Isaiah, "Those who wait upon God get fresh strength. They spread their wings and soar like eagles" (Isaiah 40:31). When we are chased and pursued, when sin and Satan are hot on our trail, we fly to Jesus. We fly to the Son who blinds our enemies with rays of light. We fly to the Christ who has flown down to earth to save us from our sins.

And one day Jesus will return to call His creatures into the clouds.

Remember, today is the tomorrow you worried about yesterday.

— **DALE CARNEGIE**

selling your soul on eBay

SOME OF US have skeletons in our closets. Others have entire cemeteries. If we live long enough, our consciences will collect the corpses of those we have hurt, lied about, and cheated on. We carry their bones with us, lugging them from class to class and place to place. We throw them in the backseat of our cars and drive them to work. We stash them in lockers at the gym. And before we go to bed, we store them in our closets and listen to their midnight rattling. Everyone carries a bag of bones. The question is, how heavy is ours?

Peggy was a girl of great faith. I'll never forget how passionately she read the Scriptures, not because she went to a Christian high school, but simply because she wanted to know God better. The pages of her Bible bled from years of inky inscriptions. Peggy and I were in the same class, the graduating class of 2000. By most standards our class was exceptional. We had the best musicians in the county, the greatest volleyball players in the area, and the finest football team in the state. But we also had a scapegoat, a girl who absorbed our frustrations and tolerated our jokes. We had an outcast, and Peggy, or "Piggy," was her name.

On the last day of finals of my sophomore year, Peggy and I shared a class. It was a math class, and the exam required a number two pencil. Having packed twelve pre-sharpened yellow pencils, I was armed to the teeth for the test. Just before the exam, Peggy, who was sitting in front of me, turned around and asked me if I had a pencil she could borrow. There was no resentment or bitterness in her voice, but without hesitation, I shook my head and lied to her. "Sorry," I said. "This is my last one." Several others followed my example and refused to give her a pencil. Some snickered at her lack of preparation. Others flat-out told her that she was going to fail. Peggy was used to the ridiculing, and she laughed it off, pretending not to care.

After the exam, Peggy got in her car and drove away. As she drove down Highway 280, her car slammed into the median, flipped onto its roof, and crashed into a pickup truck speeding in the other direction. Peggy was killed instantly, her body sent away in a bag. Only sixteen years after God gave her life, Peggy was taken home.

When the news of her death reached our high school, a blanket of guilt covered us. Everyone who had ever hurt her was instantly convicted. Our shame was thick and obvious. For months I thought about the day she died, the morning of the math exam when I refused even the simplest act of kindness. I thought about the expression on her face when she asked the teacher for something to write with after being rejected by her peers. And I thought about that pack of pencils sitting in my backpack, so new and sharp. Many nights have long since passed when Peggy's bones have rattled in my closet.

It was a difficult funeral, a time of grieving for a life cut so short.

They say Peggy looked beautiful in the coffin, her makeup flawless and her cheekbones rosy. Turns out, her real name was Margaret Elizabeth—what a beautiful name. Many students from the high school came to pay their respects to her. For most, it was a first.

I didn't go to Peggy's funeral; I wouldn't go, I couldn't go. Not after the way I had treated her. Not after the humiliation and the jokes. God took her to heaven only two hours after I gave her hell, and to this day I can't even pick up a pencil without remembering my cruelty.

You never know what you have until it's gone. For many people, Peggy was a nobody, just a face to make fun of. But God saw her differently. To God she was a somebody of great value and importance. Peggy was important not because of what she said or did, not because of how beautiful she was, not even because of how accepted or rejected she was in our high school. Peggy was important to God because she was made in His image. God minted Himself to her soul before she was born. When I made fun of Peggy, I was making fun of God.

IN SEARCH OF THE SOUL

What is a soul? Can we feel it or feed it? Can we comb it or tickle it? Is a soul just a mythological concept? Is it a figment of our imagination? Can we go to the doctor when it's sick? Can we take it out to eat when it's hungry?

The Hebrew Scriptures record that God created humans with a soul when He breathed into them. "God formed Man out of dirt from the ground and blew into his nostrils the breath of life. The Man came alive—a living soul!" (Genesis 2:7). According to God's law, the Israelites were commanded to love God with all their heart, soul, and strength (Deuteronomy 6:5).

The New Testament speaks about the soul as something distinct from the body. Jesus warned His disciples not to fear those who can kill the body but not the soul (Matthew 10:28). The apostle Peter explained that the soul can be saved through faith (1 Peter 1:9). The apostle John, while stranded on the island of Patmos, saw a vision of all the souls who for the sake of Christ were beheaded, resurrected and living with God for a thousand years (Revelation 20:4).

But how does the soul interact with the body? Leaning on Plato, Augustine underscored the distinction between body and soul. Since the soul is a different substance than the body, it continues to exist when the body is dead.[1] Relying on Aristotle, Thomas Aquinas emphasized a more unified perspective of human nature. The soul for Aquinas was so tightly tethered to the body that one is incomplete without the other. Though not a philosopher, John Calvin agreed with Augustine's view that the soul is distinct from the body and found this truth embedded in Scripture. Thus, the *Heidelberg Catechism*, which reflected this tradition, asked, "How does the resurrection of the body comfort you?" Its answer: "Not only will my soul be taken immediately after this life to Christ its head, but even my flesh, raised by the power of Christ, will be reunited with my soul and made like Christ's glorious body."[2]

Webster's dictionary defines the soul as "the immaterial essence . . . of an individual life; the spiritual essence embodied in human beings."[3] Duncan MacDougall, a twentieth-century doctor in Haverhill, Massachusetts, set out to prove Webster wrong. He believed in the physical reality of the soul, and after listening to many preachers say that the soul lives on after death, he attempted to prove scientifically that the soul has a substantial and quantifiable mass.

At the exact moment of their deaths, Dr. MacDougall weighed six dying patients and discovered that immediately after they died, each cadaver was twenty-one grams lighter. He also experimented with fifteen dogs and found that this phenomenon didn't occur in them.

According to his experiment, MacDougall proposed that the soul weighs approximately twenty-one grams and exits the body at the moment of death. His findings were published in March 1907 in the *New York Times* and in the medical journal *American Medicine*. Sadly, he did not comment on whether dogs go to heaven.

Throughout history, the soul has been researched, analyzed, and even scientifically measured, but in 2006, a soul was sold on eBay. Atheist Hemant Mehta, a twenty-three-year-old graduate student, auctioned his soul to the highest bidder. On February 3, after forty-one bids, evangelist Jim Henderson purchased the soul for five hundred and four dollars. Mr. Mehta had previously written that for each ten-dollar increment of the final bid, he would attend an hour of church services. Since then, many have tried to sell their souls on eBay, but eBay now bans such auctions. They also prohibit the sale of Nazi paraphernalia, virginity, and human organs.

> instead of asking, "what is the soul?" our quest becomes, "what do I do with my soul?"

We may never fully understand the soul. In fact, Thomas Merton wrote, "God help the man who thinks he knows all about himself."[4] But even if we cannot fully exhaust the dimensions of the soul, God holds us responsible for how we use them. Instead of asking, "What is the soul?" our quest and question becomes, "What do I do with my soul?" Do I wear my soul on my sleeve and give it to every passing passion? Do I respect it and protect it? The psalmists declared that the soul thirsts for God (Psalm 63:1), clings to God (Psalm 63:8) and rejoices after praising God (Psalm 71:23). The secret of the soul's ultimate satisfaction lies in its encounter with the God who ordained its existence.

POSTMODERNISM AND YOUR SOUL

My generation is a product of postmodernism. We are constantly taught that if there is truth, we cannot perfectly know it. Relativism is also the god of our age. It says that your interpretation of truth is no better than mine. Still worse is deconstructionism, which says, "It's not that I don't know truth; it's that I just don't care." These three mind-sets are not only tolerated in our culture; they are taught. Ironically, the only thing that's not tolerated is the person who claims that there is only one way to find absolute truth.

While postmodernism attacks the church, it has also married into it. The emerging church, as championed by Brian McLaren and others, flirts dangerously with postmodern ideology, thinking that the Christian faith must be deconstructed and then reconstructed to fit a generation that resists propositional truth. The only problem is this: The Bible is propositional. The Bible steps on toes. The Bible is offensive, unpopular, and countercultural.

I am greatly optimistic about doctrine-friendly emergents like Mark Driscoll, pastor of Mars Hill Church, Seattle, and others who retain the fundamentals of the Christian faith. They are asking the right questions—questions like "What's the identity of the church in an age of postmodernity?" and "How should Christians tailor evangelistic strategies to meet the needs of a changing generation?" These are valid questions that must be addressed. Yet there is the temptation among "doctrine-resistant" emergents to compromise biblical absolutes for feel-good, "don't step on my toes," cotton-candy Christianity. This will not only die the death of a trend, but it will also foster relativism and skepticism in the hearts of those who seek absolute truth found in the person and work of Jesus Christ.

Postmoderns have exhausted the idea that there is no meaning in life and are left longing for something more. Many churches are responding to this hunger and are communicating the message of Christ with an ardor that has been witnessed only in the great revivals of history. We want to know what God has disclosed about Himself. We want to know why we were created and how we are to behave. We want to mine the mysteries of the Maker.

PILGRIM SOULS

How should we view the soul? Are we nomads, aimlessly wandering in search of truth? Are we pedestrians, traveling without spiritual direction? Perhaps we are tourists, living for the moment, basking in the light of entertainment, popularity, and leisure.

All of us have been these things at one time or another. But God would have us be pilgrims, pilgrims with a purpose—to follow Christ wherever His steps may lead. Sometimes the trail takes us into valleys. Other times, we climb and crawl up mountains. But we can be confident that the God who blazed the trail has already traversed the trail.

The discipline of pilgrimage is a tangible reminder that we are on a journey to God. When we travel to ancient cities and sacred spots, our understanding of God increases and we begin to see our Savior through broader lenses. Some of my most spiritually challenging adventures have been in places of historical significance—like Athens and the islands of Iona (offshore Scotland) and Skellig Michael (offshore Ireland). I gained a deeper understanding of God's strength at the Rock of Gibraltar (Psalm 46:1). I saw the problem of building a house on the sand in Venice (Matthew 7:26). And the more I traveled, the more I came to understand that our journey on earth prepares us for our home in heaven.

SOULS FINDING A HOLY LOVE

Jonathan Edwards said that "it is doubtless true, and evident from these Scriptures, that the essence of all true religion lies in holy love."[5] The soul shares a two-way intimacy with God. After God invites us into His community, we crave our Creator. We pulse with passion for Him. We throb for Him. And only when our relationships, dreams, goals, opinions, wallets, and actions parallel our relationship with God can our lives gain a meaning that permeates our entire existence.

Love is a tricky thing. How do we know if we really love someone? Is it a thought or a feeling? What happens when the feeling goes away? Is it an opinion or an attitude? What happens when we change our minds? Do we love someone because they are rich or sexy? What happens when the wealth runs dry and the sex begins to fizzle instead of sizzle?

Before God destroyed the world with water, He commanded Noah to build an ark. Instead of putting leashes on animals and dragging them into the ark, each creature walked to Noah in a pair, a male and its mate (Genesis 7:9). Humans, too, were created with a mate. Henri Nouwen suggests:

> We probably have wondered in our many lonesome moments if there is one corner in this competitive, demanding world where it is safe to be relaxed, to expose ourselves to someone else, and to give unconditionally. It might be very small and hidden. But if this corner exists, it calls for a search through the complexities of our human relationships in order to find it.[6]

I am persuaded that there is a mate for us to walk with. For some it is a marriage relationship. For others, a deep friendship. The soul was made for companionship, and God Himself communes with us and brings us into the ark of salvation.

○ ○ ○ ○ ○ ○

A boy once made a boat. It was a special boat, a red, shiny boat. For days he sketched its design, measured its dimensions, and carved its frame. He carefully crafted the mast, whittled a rudder, and glued the mast to the hull. With meticulous care, he even tied pieces of twine together and strung them along the boat's perimeter. It lacked only one thing. Picking up a paintbrush, the boy signed his name on its side and declared that this was the best boat ever created.

One sunny Saturday, the boy decided to sail the boat in a river. The water upheld the vessel as it floated by the banks. The boy was thrilled. There was his creation, his pride and joy, handling the currents and rapids of the river. But then, to the boy's horror, the boat crashed against the rocks and drifted out of sight. After hours of searching, the boy was heartbroken and returned to his house without his beautiful boat.

Several days later, the boy was walking down the street and saw his boat displayed in a window. He couldn't believe his eyes and ran inside the shop.

"That's my boat," he yelled. "Give me back my boat!"

"Are you sure about that?" the shop owner said.

The boy nodded. "Yes, I'm sure. Look, there's my signature on the side."

"That might be your signature," the man said, "but if you want this boat, you have to buy it." He pointed to the price tag hanging from the rudder. It cost a lot. But the boy reached into his pocket, pulled out everything he had, and purchased back the boat he had made.

Christians belong to God by creation and redemption. In Him we were made and remade, formed and reformed. King David wrote, "Oh yes, you shaped me first inside, then out; you formed me in my mother's womb" (Psalm 139:15). And though we fell from original perfection and were sold to sin, Christ died a criminal's death to buy us back. Everything in the syllabus of salvation happened just the way God wrote it, and with Paul the apostle we pray that the eyes of our hearts may be enlightened in order that we will know the hope and riches of God's inheritance for His saints (Ephesians 1:18).

○ ○ ○ ○ ○ ○

At the end of the day, the soul asks three questions: So what? Who cares? Why not? These questions splash against us, wearing and tearing, corroding our cores. We ask the question, "So what?" What's the meaning of my life? What's the point of it all? "Who cares?" Is there anyone who gives a rip? "Why not?" Would anyone notice if I died?

Questions like these have exciting answers. God gives us passions for holiness that combat our passions for wickedness. He gives us a faith that fights temptation. And not only that, He gives us Himself. Jesus said, "Are you tired? Worn out? Burned out on religion? Come to Me. Get away with Me and you'll recover your life. I'll show you how to take a real rest" (Matthew 11:28). We relax in the knowledge of God's affection for us and His presence in us.

SOULS IN SERVICE

We also rest in the comforts of the community God has given us. Christians are created not only for fellowship with Christ, but also with His body—men and women, boys and girls who are believers who care for one another. Paul wrote, "In this way we are like the various parts of a human body. Each part gets its meaning from the body as a whole, not the other way around" (Romans 12:4–5). Therefore, if the foot is sore, our hand should soothe it. If the hand is cold, our breath should warm it. Paul also wrote, "Stoop down and reach out to those who are oppressed" (Galatians 6:2).

The word *compassion* is made up of the Latin words *com* and *passio*, meaning "to suffer with." Jesus set a supreme example on how to suffer with us, and we are called to mimic His pattern.

The soul that serves both Christ and His body cannot be sold on eBay. It cannot be bartered or stolen. It cannot be erased from the blackboard of providence. It's so fixed within God's fingers that not a hand from the pit of hell can reach up and pull it to the flames. A cocoon surrounds the Christians whom God saves, and we are forever sheltered by grace, protected by mercy, and preserved by love.

Salvation is not a staircase filled with souls that climb to God. We stand not on a ladder but on an escalator—God pulls us to Himself, moment by moment and day by day. He takes our grime and gives us grace. He takes our filth and gives us faith. And on this highway to heaven, our souls find meaning. We begin to see ourselves as targets of God's unconditional love, and God the Creator grows bigger in our eyes. Since we didn't earn our salvation, we can't lose it. Since we cannot buy our freedom, it cannot be sold. We are God's paintings, and God never abandons His work. His signature is signed on our souls and we belong to Him. He took the mess we were and makes us into masterpieces that are worthy to be hung in the galleries of glory.

○ ○ ○ ○ ○ ○

Peggy's soul is with God, but I still carry her bones with me. From the grave she speaks, whispering words of forgiveness in my ear. "Father, forgive him," she says, "for he knows not what he does." Every time I want to make fun of someone, I hear her voice. Every time I laugh at the clown who drops his tray in the cafeteria, I remember her gentleness. And one day, when death does what death does best, I will see her again. On some golden avenue or silver alleyway I will find her. And there will be an apology on my lips, and a pencil in my hand.

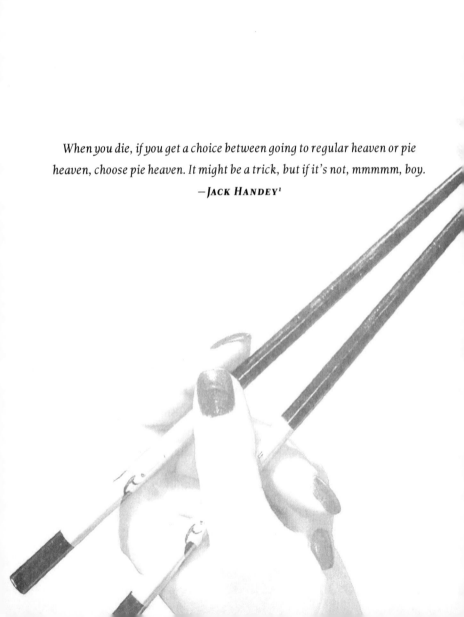

When you die, if you get a choice between going to regular heaven or pie heaven, choose pie heaven. It might be a trick, but if it's not, mmmmm, boy.

—**JACK HANDEY**[1]

from milk
to meat

IT WAS A small church, the kind that smells of hickory and history. The pews were hard, the pulpit massive, and aqua-blue light poured through the jagged stained-glass window. This was the kind of church I didn't mind visiting. In years to come I would speak in many white-steepled churches growing in the middle of some green Alabama pasture. I rather love them, so quaint and quiet. But today I was a visitor to this church, not a speaker, and I took my seat near the back of the sanctuary.

It was my junior year in high school, and God was strangely warming my heart. I wanted to know about other denominations within the body of Christ, and a friend joined me for the experience. We sat in the back of this church, preparing our hearts for worship.

The music was unfamiliar but exciting. People were shouting to Jesus, running up and down the aisles, laughing, crying, jumping, screaming, and some were even waving their arms and chirping like birds. I looked at my friend, whose eyes were as wide as mine.

For my whole life I've been very careful not to criticize the work of the Lord. In the book of Acts God accomplished great things and His kingdom spread throughout the world. I strongly believe that God gives spiritual gifts to different limbs beneath the head of Christ, but never had I encountered such emotion in a worship service. I tried to clap along but was distracted by the woman in front of us barking like a dog as she jumped up and down.

After the singing ceased, the pastor walked to the pulpit. His suit was shiny and impressive, his boots polished and pointy. I couldn't wait to hear what he had to say. He took as his text Job 42:12: "The LORD blessed the latter part of Job's life more than the first. He had fourteen thousand sheep, six thousand camels, a thousand yoke of oxen and a thousand donkeys" (NIV).

> "Jesus can pay your bills, give you promotions, and buy you new cars."

After reading the passage, he put down the Bible and reached into his coat pocket. He fidgeted for several seconds and then pulled out a golden pocket watch with a long chain attached to it. Holding it before the congregation, he said, "This is an $800 watch, one of the finest of its kind. It was hand-crafted by a company in Switzerland, and the Bible verse we just read is going to teach you how to afford one."

I looked at my friend. He shared my disbelief. *God wants us to be rich?* Perhaps this was just a preacher joke intended to warm up the congregation. Every speaker needs an icebreaker.

He continued. "The book of Job is about money. You want to be rich, don't you?"

The church members nodded.

"In the Old Testament," he said, "God blessed His people with riches because that was how He showed them His love. The same is true today, and I want to tell you this morning that Jesus Christ can fill your wallets if you are faithful to Him. He can pay your bills, give you promotions, and buy you new cars."

The congregation gave a loud "amen" and applauded. After a thirty-minute sermon about Job's life and how God blessed him, several people approached the altar. Suddenly, the pastor looked right at my friend and me and invited us to join him in the front. We didn't want to, but we obeyed. With music playing in the background, he asked if we had the gift of tongues. I didn't know about my friend, but I sure didn't.

"Stop the music," the pastor said. "We have two visitors who need the Holy Spirit today." Everyone gathered in a large circle around us as the pastor attempted to give us the gift of tongues. Placing his hand on our stomachs, he told us to close our eyes. Then he commanded his congregation to blow on us. One by one, each person came by and blew directly at our faces; some of them were only inches away. I tried to hold my breath and avoid the germs, but it was difficult to time my breaths because my eyes were closed.

"What sin in your life is keeping you from receiving the Holy Spirit?" the pastor demanded.

Hmm. Not sure.

When everyone saw that I wasn't speaking in tongues, they grew more fervent and eventually angry. The blowing got harder, and some even slapped me on the back. One guy put his hand on my forehead and tried to push me over. Having seen this on television, I knew that I was supposed to fall, but he wasn't pushing hard enough to knock me over, and I didn't sense the Holy Spirit taking me to the ground. So there I stood.

"Sin," the preacher yelled, "in the name of the Lord, I command you to come out of this boy!" With everyone yelling, groaning, chirping, and barking, I peeked over at my friend, whose lips were moving. He later told me that he faked it.

After fifteen minutes of this, the pastor threw his hands in the air and told me that I wasn't a Christian. He rebuked me in front of the whole congregation, saying that the Holy Ghost wanted nothing to do with me. He told me to repent of my sins before I came back. Sad and confused, I left.

MAKING JESUS SEXY

Throughout the history of Christianity, people have been removed from churches for many reasons. Some were kicked out for political issues, others for doctrinal matters. In the medieval era, there are even accounts of eighty-six animal excommunications, including insects and caterpillars.[2] Now, I'm no insect, but I did feel like one crawling out of that sanctuary. That was the only time I've ever felt excommunicated from a Protestant church, and though I never went back to that congregation, I do remember them in my prayers. I had a seminary professor who once told me that the Christian life "is not about a gospel of prosperity; it's about prospering the gospel."[3] And as bizarre as the whole experience was, especially the barking and chirping, it forced me to develop a biblical theology of God and His church.

When the apostle Paul wrote to the Christians in Corinth, he recognized that they were spiritual babies. In his letter to them he wrote, "You're acting like infants in relation to Christ, capable of nothing much more than nursing at the breast" (1 Corinthians 3:2). The church in Corinth was packed with problems. For starters, many of the Christians were participating in incest, prostitution, and wrongful lawsuits. There were also divisions and quarrellings in the church. Some followed Paul, others Peter. Since Corinth was a city where sev-

eral trade routes intersected, it became a place of commerce and immorality, a playpen of sin for spiritual infants.

Only babies should be breast-fed. It would seem odd, if not
downright disgusting, for adults to suck milk from breasts. But em-
barrassingly enough, many of us in the church are sucking spiritual
milk from pastors and teachers long after our stomachs can handle
meat. We live in a Corinth culture and have adopted many of its prac-
tices. Instead of eating broccoli and chicken, we drown ourselves in
the buttermilk of biblical ignorance. With hands outstretched, we
reach for a cookie Christianity that is dipped in the milk of spiritual
immaturity.

A. W. Tozer, a prophetic writer and thinker, wrote that religion
rises only as high as its view of God.[4] A low view of God leads to a low
view of worship. Those who were born in the '80s and '90s are called
generation Y. This is my generation. We were always told that we were
special. If we picked up a spoon, we were special. If we went to the
bathroom, we were special. It didn't matter what our IQ or grades,
we were special anyway. Girls grew up thinking they were prin-
cesses; boys thought they were princes. When we were thirsty, we
screamed. When we were hungry, we yelled. And every person existed to rock our cribs and kiss our heads. The whole world revolved
around us—our needs, our wants, and our rights. Since royalty gets
whatever it wants, we became convinced that we were the center of
the universe.

Our spiritual lives were no different. Most of us think we are the
center of our salvation, the highlight of our hymns, and how lucky
of God to love and serve us. But the world doesn't revolve around us
any more than the sun revolves around the moon. Before we were
ever created, God found pleasure in Himself. He was wholly complete
without us. Our view of God must be corrected—we have thought too

lowly of Him. We want a Jesus genie we can rub the right way in order to get our own way.

But worship is not about us; it's not about the love we feel when we love the way we love God. Yes, we are important to God, important enough to die for. But we must abandon the notion that God needs us to help accomplish His will. Though it feels unnatural to worship a God who does not worship us, we must divorce ourselves from thinking that God can't bring people into His church without our help. We build Him gyms, throw concerts, and keep our sermons short and nonconfrontational. We are terrified about offending anyone, and thus the church looks like the world in order to draw the world into the church. We must make Jesus sexy.

Worship, however, is about God—His passions and interests. It's about His power and pleasure. Reality exists for Him. *We* exist for Him. And when our lives are tuned to His praise, when we readjust our thinking, we find freedom in focusing our gaze on something greater than ourselves. And we grow to love the God who revolves around Himself.

It's a dangerous thing to bore a powerful God.

When Christianity first took root in the first century, the pagan temples in Alexandria and other cities used technology to bring people into the shrines. Sophisticated machines that made thunder and opened doors dazzled the world and instilled fear for the gods into the people. But Christians have no need for these things. Jesus once said, "And I, as I am lifted up from the earth, will attract everyone to me" (John 12:32). The problem that Paul experienced in Corinth, and our problem today, is that Jesus Christ is not lifted up. He isn't trusted as the marvelous magnet that draws people to Himself. In many churches He's still lying in the tomb, wrapped in linens and waiting to be warmed.

CHRIST THE GREAT WARRIOR AND SHEPHERD

But the Scriptures paint Him in another light. Jesus Christ is the great warrior who grabbed the dragon's tail and slammed him down to earth. He is the loving shepherd who tears wild bears apart when they threaten His flock. And unlike Samson, there are no kryptonite scissors to drain Christ's power. When John was on the Isle of Patmos, he saw a mighty vision of Christ: "Then I saw heaven open wide—and oh! a white horse and its Rider. The Rider, named Faithful and True, judges and makes war in pure righteousness. His eyes are a blaze of fire, on his head many crowns" (Revelation 19:11–12). In other words, Christ isn't an impotent husband who needs Viagra to accomplish His will. He can satisfy His bride better than that. He is the mighty Rock of Ages. That's why the most seeker-friendly strategy a church can implement is the elevation and exaltation of Jesus Christ.

When King David fled his palace because his son Absalom wanted to kill him, he wrote, "Many are saying of me, 'God will not deliver him.' But you are a shield around me, O Lord; you bestow glory on me and lift up my head" (Psalm 3:2–3 NIV). The Hebrew word for "glory" means heavy, weighty, or significant. In fact it comes from the same word group as "liver," the heaviest organ in the body (approximately three pounds). When we speak of God's glory, we acknowledge His heaviness and importance.

When the Israelites set up camp, they always put the temple at its center. For them, the presence of God was sacred; it was a holy space where God lived. That is why David wrote, "I love the house where you live, O Lord, the place where your glory dwells" (Psalm 26:8 NIV). Once a year a priest entered the Holy of Holies to offer a sacrifice for the sins of the people, and a rope was tied to him so he could be pulled back in case the glory of the living Lord killed him.

Job probably wet his pants when he got a glimpse of God's glory.

God gave Satan the green light to steal Job's cattle. Then went his gems—the Devil huffed and puffed and blew a house down on Job's kids, and it was too much for him to take. He tore his clothes, shaved his head, and fell to the ground in worship.

Worship? How could a man who lost everything except a wife who told him to "curse God and be done with it" (Job 2:9) fall to the ground in worship? Famine replaced wealth, sickness replaced health, yet Job declared, "God gives, God takes. God's name be ever blessed" (Job 1:21). Later in the book, Job struggled to reconcile God's purpose with his pain, and he sought to argue his case before God. He wanted to talk with God, to converse with his Creator. And to his surprise, God talked back. "Pull yourself together, Job. Up on your feet! Stand tall! I have some questions for you, and I want some straight answers. Where were you when I created the earth? Tell me, since you know so much! Who decided on its size? Certainly you'll know that!" (Job 38:3–5).

> God wouldn't have lost an ounce of glory if the great flood had destroyed everyone, including Noah.

Job answered: "I'm speechless, in awe—words fail me. I should never have opened my mouth! I've talked too much, way too much. I'm ready to shut up and listen" (Job 40:4–5). Job remembered that he had never numbered the stars, scattered the darkness, or told the ocean where to flow. He never created a bird, hitchhiked the galaxy, or tied Orion's belt around his waist. But God had. And Job learned that God's arm was bigger than his and God's glory was much heavier than his own. It is true that in the end of the book, God restored Job's health and wealth, but the theme of the book isn't about gaining financial independence or buying golden pocket watches, but rather developing a view of God as the Creator who sovereignly works His will even through pain and suffering.

What does it mean for God to be sovereign? I asked a youth group this question once and was shocked by the response. A guy in the back of the room said, "It means that God can do whatever the hell he wants."

I grinned. "Yeah, that's one way to put it."

But he had a point. The owner has the right to throw away the inventory, and God wouldn't have lost an ounce of glory if the great flood had destroyed everyone, including Noah. But God in His grace *became* the inventory to purchase our lives with His blood. The Creator became the creation, and according to Revelation 13:8, in the mind of God Jesus Christ was crucified to the cross before the world was spinning on its axis. The veil of the temple that once separated us from God's presence has been torn in two, and both prostitute and peasant have access to the Holy of Holies.

Paul told the Corinthian church, "In the Messiah, in Christ, God leads us from place to place in one perpetual victory parade. Through us, he brings knowledge of Christ. Everywhere we go, people breathe in the exquisite fragrance. Because of Christ, we give off a sweet scent rising to God, which is recognized by those on the way of salvation" (2 Corinthians 2:14–15). Most of the time, however, I smell like a rat and not a rose. But in His love He accepts my praise and hears my prayer. And He accomplishes His perfect plan for my life in spite of me.

a revival is breaking out among younger evangelicals who proclaim God's heaviness and worship Him in glory.

God is the author, editor, and publisher of our lives. In Him we are written and distributed to a world that needs the good news of the gospel of Christ. But a day is coming when the Lord will reclaim

His library books and Christ will return to earth, not as a servant but as a king.

Make no mistake about it: The gospel is an offensive animal. It tears apart pride and tells us we are fundamentally corrupted. It shreds independence, rips open chest cavities, and replaces hearts of stone with hearts of flesh. It even slices through skulls and exchanges worldly minds for minds of Christ.

Every Christian is a theologian. You don't need a beard, a pipe, and a library to think about God. In fact, everyone has a theology. Some people think God doesn't exist. That's a theology. Others think if He did exist we couldn't know Him. That's a theology too. Every action is based on a theology. At the end of the day, our theology of God exists for our relationship with God. Our thoughts about God lead us into a deeper worship of God. And a day is coming when the Great Liver—the Glory that is heavy—will filter wheat from chaff, sheep from goats, saved from lost. But those who love God with head and heart will be ushered into an eternity where God's loving presence pervades not only the city, but also our souls.

These days, I sense a growing desire within my generation to lift up Christ and see His glory as something sacred again. A revival is breaking out among younger evangelicals who proclaim God's heaviness and worship Him in glory. We are tired of elevating ourselves with self-centered worship. We are recognizing the awesome and powerful name of God, a name so holy that ancient scribes would bathe before writing it. We are burning off our spiritual cellulite, exercising our spiritual muscles, and praising God in spirit and truth.

We are instruments in the Musician's hand, and God is preparing to play up a storm. We are taking forks and knives to the Scriptures and exchanging milky mustaches for substantial cuts of christological meat. And we're enjoying the five-course meal. I sense a craving in our churches and youth groups for a deeper union with Christ. A renewal movement is at work within our nation, a movement of reconciliation with God. In our nation's short history there have been two great awakenings, and I believe the third is rising in the water. The water has come ashore, and soon it will splash across our desert land.

SPITTING OUT COTTON-CANDY CHRISTIANITY

God is always at work in this world. Throughout history, His church has never died the death of a fad, even though it usually was the minority movement. The flame was never extinguished. As seen in movements like Louie Giglio's Passion conferences, college kids and young adults are aching for authentic worship, and it's transcending denominations and traditions. We agree with Paul: "When I was a child, I talked like a child, I thought like a child, I reasoned like a child. When I became a man, I put childish ways behind me" (1 Corinthians 13:11 NIV). We are spitting out a cotton-candy Christianity that melts in our mouths and poisons our souls. We want meat. Not charred steak, but juicy rib eyes that still contain the blood of Christ.

God's church does not look the same everywhere, but we are all members of the body of Christ. We appreciate other limbs, like Anglican elbows and Lutheran legs, and the denominational differences are important, but we keep them below the surface of the Communion table because we all embrace the teachings of the Reformation—grace alone, faith alone, and Scripture alone. Other traditions within the branches of Christianity contribute to its trunk and give us insights into our own faith. If only we could hunger for holiness like Franciscans, work and pray like Benedictines, evangelize like Baptists, pray like Presbyterians, and sing like Wesleyans. If our love for God doesn't unite us, certainly our fear of Satan should. Our enemy is far greater than our differences.

To belong to a denomination is to belong to a city. But one who lives in a city also lives in a state. And one who lives in a state also lives in a country. Our Christian faith is local and universal, narrow and broad. We must not limit on earth what God ordains for heaven.

And above all else, we must lift up Jesus Christ, the lighthouse of the world and the hope of our salvation. For only He can splash our dehydrated Christianity with His presence and give us meat to go with our spiritual milk.

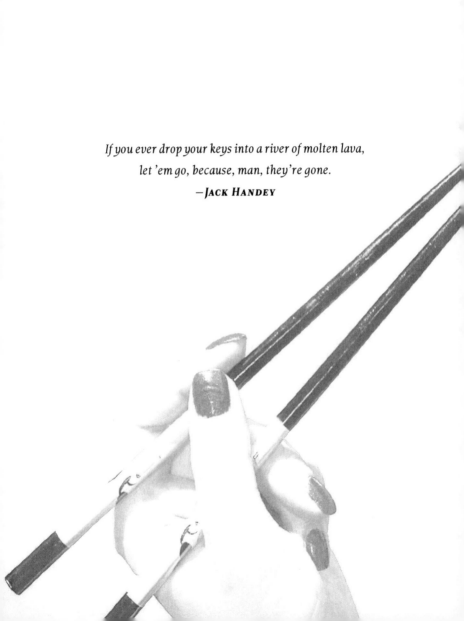

If you ever drop your keys into a river of molten lava,
let 'em go, because, man, they're gone.

—JACK HANDEY

hollow places

IN THE EARLY afternoon of August 24, A.D. 79, a seventeen-year-old boy named Pliny looked seventeen miles across the Bay of Naples and saw a vertical black cloud rising twenty miles into the air. It was jutting from the top of Mount Vesuvius on the southwestern coast of Italy. In his own words, "A fearful black cloud was rent by forked and quivering bursts of flame . . . like flashes of lightning magnified in size."[1] Pliny's uncle, a natural scientist, sought to examine the phenomenon, but when he learned that a woman named Rectina was in danger at the foot of Vesuvius, he set out to rescue her in a boat. He never came back.

Meanwhile, volcanic ash covered the sky for miles around and even stretched as far as Constantinople, Turkey. According to Pliny, the black column rising from Vesuvius collapsed and covered the sea. The Roman cities of Pompeii and Herculaneum didn't stand a chance.

They lay at the foot of the volcano, bowing down before its sovereign summit. But soon their altar would produce earthquakes, twenty feet of ash, and a pyroclastic flow—a 932-degree Fahrenheit, ground-hugging avalanche of hot ash, gas, and rocks traveling at sixty-two miles per hour.

As the dense cloud rushed toward them, Pliny grabbed the hand of his mother, and together they fled for their lives. "We had scarcely sat down to rest," he wrote, "when darkness fell, not the dark of a moonless or cloudy night, but as if the lamp had been put out in a closed room. . . . Many besought the aid of the gods, but still more imagined there were no gods left, and that the universe was plunged into eternal darkness for evermore."[2] After the darkness thinned, Pliny and his mother scurried back to Misenum to await news about his uncle. No one had expected this mountain to explode because a few decades earlier, in A.D. 20, the geographer Strabone said that Vesuvius was extinct.[3]

Previous volcanic activity had nourished the soil around Pompeii, four crops were harvested annually and home gardens overflowed with fruit and flowers. Before the eruption, the peace of the Roman Empire fostered military laziness, the walls around the city deteriorated, and immorality saturated the city. Brothels, homosexuality, and pornographic mosaics filled the streets.

Pliny's account of the eruption of Mount Vesuvius was doubted and mocked during the Middle Ages. The very existence of Pompeii was forgotten, but in 1748 accidental discoveries led to an investigation and eventually a dig. In 1860, Giuseppe Fiorelli became the director of the excavations, and he methodically uncovered the well-preserved city.

As Fiorelli dug, he came across hollow places in the thick layer of volcanic ash. Not knowing what they were, he continued digging through them. But then he had an idea. He mixed a plaster together and poured it into each cavity he encountered. After the plaster dried, he carefully uncovered the ash and was shocked at what he saw.

Bodies. Some were curled in the fetal position; other victims had covered their heads with their hands and arms. These were people who lived during the time of the apostles Peter and Paul. There was even a dog that had died wrestling against its chain. They had been killed instantly from the heat and gases of the volcano. After their bodies decayed, a hollow space was all that remained, and the plaster that filled these spaces preserved the last minute of their lives. The horrified expressions on their faces are forever minted in time. It was an eerie discovery, a snapshot of the brutality of nature and the mortality of man.

INVISIBLE PLEASURES

In the summer of 2006, I traveled through Italy with my in-laws and my wife. It was a pilgrimage of Italian proportion—we slept in monasteries, visited ancient churches, and climbed the leaning tower of Pisa. Of course, we had to make room for our daily quota of gelato (hazelnut, please).

From Naples we boarded the train to Pompeii. It was a slow ride that stopped at every city on the coast, but the trip was worth the trouble. Upon arrival, I was immediately impressed by the sheer size of ancient Pompeii. This wasn't a small village with a handful of huts; rather, the city was spread out and complete with all the Roman trappings—adorned temples, bathhouses, and even an amphitheater where up to five thousand people could watch gladiators in combat. I walked the ancient roads, dragging my jaw behind me. The ash of Mount Vesuvius had perfectly preserved the architecture.

Though dating back almost two millennia, the streets of Pompeii looked as they had then. Indeed, to walk on them is to journey into the past. We passed the Temple of Vespasian and the House of Faun. We saw the outdoor swimming pool, the bakeries along the street, and even a public bathroom.

But when we arrived at the garden of the fugitives, I'll never forget the sight—plastered remains of refugees who had died trying to escape the eruption. In total, the forms of thirteen figures were displayed, including six children.[4] Their bodies were curled up and some clutched their throats. After studying these pitiful, stony creatures, I turned around to look at Mount Vesuvius. It stood tall against the horizon, almost proudly, and for a brief moment I was reminded that it could erupt again. It has blown several times since A.D. 79, and perhaps I too would become trapped in ash, hollowed out by generations of the future.

I once had a Sunday school teacher who taught me that I had a God-sized hole in my heart that only Christ could fill—a hollow place, a vacuum that cannot be satisfied with drugs, sex, or money. In search of this emptiness, I went to the Bible. I searched the prophets in the Old Testament and the Gospels in the New. I looked from Genesis to Jude for evidence of this empty organ but found nothing.

Turns out I wasn't as empty or neutral as I thought. My organs were eaten with rebellion against God. The hollow theory was a myth, and the Scripture informed me that I was coated with the cancer of sin. King David declared, "All have turned aside, they have together become corrupt; there is no one who does good, not even one" (Psalm 14:3 NIV).

A friend once asked me what I would do if I were invisible. Not just sort of transparent, or kind of hazy, but altogether invisible to the naked eye. I gave it some thought. Perhaps I would haunt my friends. Rob a bank. Or sneak into the girls' locker room. Perhaps I would become the ultimate spy or the ultimate foot soldier. If there were no consequences or limits, there's no telling what I would do. And so I told my friend my secret. It was a dirty deed, almost unforgivable. But he didn't raise his eyebrows too highly; his wasn't much cleaner than mine.

No one is hollow. Even the men, women, and children of Pompeii, with their telltale cavities, had bodies filled with organs as well as sins. And today, the most gracious gentleman who escorts grandmothers across the street battles his secret sins. Even the most adorable grandmother who knits sweaters for her grandchildren wages war with pride and gossip.

we want our sins to be "mistakes." everyone makes mistakes!

All of us do. We all have really juicy answers to the question, "What would you do if you were invisible?" Why? Because we are depraved by default. Paul says, "For as in Adam all die" (1 Corinthians 15:22 NIV).

But we don't like that. Being told that we are fundamentally damaged rubs us the wrong way. We don't like to use the word *sin* because it doesn't cater to our pride. We want our sins to be "mistakes." Everyone makes mistakes! Mistakes are forgivable. But sins paint us too darkly. We want to be perfect, but if we aren't, then at least really good. We want to be really good, but if we aren't, then at least somewhat kind. We want to be somewhat kind, but if we aren't, then at least mildly ill. We want to be mildly ill, but if we aren't, then at least fully conscious. And so on. But if we examine the Bible, we discover that we are not just injured or even caught in a coma. We are *dead*. "As for you, you were dead in your transgressions and sins" (Ephesians 2:1 NIV). And not just any kind of dead, but smelly, decaying dead.

Those who have not been made alive by Christ lie motionless on the ground. And demons, like vultures, circle the world, taking bits of flesh from their bodies. Those who don't know God are as lifeless as those refugees at Pompeii trying to flee the wrath to come. But Paul reminds us, "When God lives and breathes in you . . . you are delivered from that dead life. With his Spirit living in you, your body will be as alive as Christ's!" (Romans 8:10). And the Great Fisher of Men places Christians in the water and gives life to our shriveled scales.

The great reformer Martin Luther once said, "If I rest, I rust." No doubt he was a busy man—upholding biblical truths, defending arguments against opponents, and translating the Scriptures from Greek and Hebrew into the common German language. But God invites us to slow down and engage the quiet moments of our day. He invites us to hollow out the hollow hours of our lives and sense His presence. As we pour the plaster into the sacred spaces, we will discover treasures beyond our expectation.

> since God gave us brains big enough to know how small they really are, we must embrace the hollow places with humility.

Have you ever pondered the deep mysteries of God? For example, how do we explain the Trinity? How can one person be three people at the same time? How did Jesus walk on water? Did the water have an identity crisis and act like earth? What about the incarnation? How did the infinite God become a man of blood and bone? Did Mary just wake up to find a divine loaf of bread baking in her oven?

In my college days, I heard a professor in the religion department deny the validity of the miracles. He was trained in the historical-critical method and believed that if science couldn't explain the miracles of God, then he couldn't embrace them as true. If he couldn't comprehend how Jesus fed five thousand people with a sack lunch and a prayer, he dismissed it. And I remember him saying something to the effect of, "The Bible is a book of myths. They aren't bad myths, but in our post-enlightened mind-set, we cannot take them seriously." His words were golden for students who had no experience with Christianity, and he uprooted the faith of those who were not firmly planted. But Jesus once said, "If anyone causes one of these little ones who believe in me to sin, it would be better for him to be thrown into the sea with a large millstone tied around his neck" (Mark 9:42 NIV). And I sat in class, thinking about heaven's rock quarry.

Christians don't know how God split the Red Sea, flooded the world, healed the sick, or raised the dead. We don't know how Jesus withered the fig tree or calmed the storm. We certainly don't know how many angels can stand on the head of a pin. But one thing we do know, and of this we can be sure: The God who created reality can tweak it whenever He wants to. The beauty of faith dwells in the substance of mystery, and if we start throwing out miracles we must also abandon the work of the cross, the greatest miracle of all.

There will always remain question marks. This is why God doesn't let us walk by sight, for now we see through a dark mirror (1 Corinthians 13:12). Since God gave us brains big enough to know how small they really are, we must embrace the hollow places with humility and faith. Yet the God who packed His Word with truth gives us strength to excavate its riches. According to Martin Luther, the Bible is the "best and purest treasure, as a mine full of great wealth, which can never be exhausted . . . ."[5] But when we pour the plaster, our thirst for Him grows and our constant digging gives us the stamina we need for greater fellowship with our Father.

THE DANGER OF DOUBT

Thomas struggled with doubt. During the life and ministry of Jesus, he saw Christ performing miracles and touching lepers. He was a disciple, after all. He saw lives that were changed and people forgiven. But no matter how many people Jesus touched, Thomas still did not believe. After Jesus arose from the dead, the disciples who saw Christ tried to convince Thomas that He was alive. But Thomas said, "Unless I see the nail holes in his hands, put my finger in the nail holes,

there's no room in the life of a Christian for "I think I can."

and stick my hand in his side, I won't believe it" (John 20:25). A week later, Jesus appeared in a room with the disciples and said to Thomas, "Take your finger and examine my hands. Take your hand and stick it in my side. Don't be unbelieving. Believe" (John 20:27). And when Thomas gazed upon the hollow of the Holy, his eyes were opened to the truth.

Doubts can be dangerous. They threaten to wash us from the Rock of Ages by suggesting we never stood on it to begin with. I sometimes think that God only demands a little mustard seed of my faith to move a mountain. But I've never moved a pebble, much less an alp.

Not too long ago I was watching a morning edition of Fox News and they were showing a picture of Mount Everest from a satellite in outer space. Mount Everest is the tallest mountain in the world, a whopping 29,028 feet above sea level. Yet from the satellite's perspective, it looked more like a molehill than a mountain. It was almost two dimensional, a wart on the surface of the earth's skin. And if He wanted to, God could've taken His tweezers and dug it out of the ground. The whole earth is a fragile marble, floating through time and space. And if we can raise our perspective high enough, we can see that it's not our faith that moves the mountain; it's the God behind our faith who does the work.

When I was a child, I loved the story about the little engine that could. He was a determined choo-choo train that faced an enormous obstacle. As he proceeded along his tracks, he encountered a mountain in the way. Up and up he went. The steam was spewing and the wheels were racing, but the engine began to lose assurance that he would make it to his destination. He said to himself, "I think I can, I think I can, I think I can!" The weight of the world lay heavily on his back. But he kept saying, "I think I can, I think I can, I think I can!"

But there's no room in the life of a Christian for "I think I can." Simon Peter didn't say, "You are the Christ, the son of the living God, I *think*." Jesus Christ didn't say, "I am the way, the truth, and the life, *just maybe*." Good for Job, who said, "I *know* that my Redeemer lives, and that in the end he will stand upon the earth" (Job 19:25 NIV, emphasis added). The man born blind said, "I don't know everything about this Jesus who healed me. I don't have a Ph.D. in christology. I haven't memorized the levitical law. But one thing I know: I once was blind but now I see" (author paraphrase of John 9:25).

THE ABSCESS KNOWN AS POMPEII

In Crocs and flip-flops, my wife and I trudged up the side of Mount Vesuvius, wishing a train could take us to the top. An engine would have really helped our hike. Having walked through Pompeii all day, our legs were tired and our energy was low. Though it was summer, a storm was blowing across the summit of the volcano, and freezing rain found its way to the driest parts of my body. The whole ordeal was like trekking through a shower of hostile Dip 'n Dots. Occasionally the wind let up and we continued on the trail, but then it rushed back and assaulted the weary umbrella in our hands. I heard myself think, *God, an eruption right now wouldn't be so bad.*

For a few minutes, the clouds thinned and we looked down at the valley below. Dark trails of solidified lava streaked the side of the hill, lava from a previous eruption. It was a moment of awe, a moment when I realized how small and helpless I really was. Miles below our feet, lava churned like acid in the stomach of the beast, and Rebecca and I leaned over the edge to look inside the crater of its mouth. Our limbs were shaking and our toes were numb, but we peeked at the center of Vesuvius and took a picture.

When I was in high school, I had a wisdom tooth pulled. Actually, they didn't pull it out; they cut it from my jawbone. It was about as pleasant as it sounds. After the surgery, the hollow pocket abscessed and became infected. My friends called me "chipmunk cheeks," and it amazed me how something so hollow could bring such grief and torture.

> God preserves His pilgrim souls with unconditional love— a lava-hot love that ignites our zeal for Christ.

Seventeen years before Vesuvius abscessed, a severe earthquake shook the land. It was not a mild tremor; rather, its vibration destroyed much of Pompeii. Six hundred sheep died that day, and many people lost their sanity.[6] Interestingly enough, on his journey to Rome, the apostle Paul traveled through this area within a year or two of this earthquake. Having sailed from Sicily, Paul arrived at Puteoli, a port town on the north end of the Bay of Naples, only forty miles from Pompeii. Puteoli was the first Roman port in this area, founded in 194 B.C., and became popular for its hot springs, which the Romans believed could cure illnesses. Paul discovered a Christian community here and stayed with them for seven days (Acts 28:14). Though there's no evidence that he traveled to Pompeii, Paul certainly saw Mount Vesuvius.

As Rebecca and I stumbled down the side of the volcano, I thought of Paul as he passed through this region. What would he have told the

Christians in Pompeii if there was a church there? Would he have addressed their brothels, idols, and pornography?

What would Paul have written to the church in America? My country is filled with pluralism and immorality. Entertainment is the god of our age, and we regularly tithe to its ministry. While we don't have a Vesuvius in our backyard, we do have a Yellowstone. Scientists who study Yellowstone National Park suggest pressurized gases and magma stir beneath the surface, and that any eruption would scatter ash from Wyoming to Mississippi. If that zit were ever squeezed, the world as we know it would not be the same.

The apostle Peter warned that "God decreed destruction for the cities of Sodom and Gomorrah. A mound of ashes was all that was left—grim warning to anyone bent on an ungodly life. . . . So God knows how to rescue the godly from evil trials" (2 Peter 2:6, 9). This world is not void of troubles, but Christians can be confident that God preserves His pilgrim souls with unconditional love—a lava-hot love that ignites our zeal for Christ and melts our hearts of ice. We have hope that the God who formed us from dust informs us with truth, and one day He will transform us with glory. And we will forever be absorbed into the hollow of His heart.

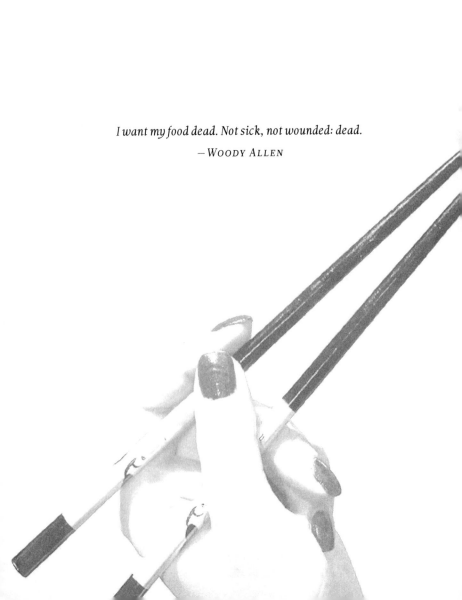

I want my food dead. Not sick, not wounded: dead.

—WOODY ALLEN

sushi faith

MY TEETH sank into the cold, slimy fish. It was slippery on the tongue and sickening to the taste. The entire table of Japanese hosts watched as I tried to force the bite down. I had to think of a plan. Perhaps I could swallow it whole, quickly ending the oily ordeal. Perhaps I could store it in my cheeks for later. All eyes awaited my decision, but my mouth wouldn't obey. My stomach begged me not to swallow, and my throat swore revenge if I did.

Traditional Japanese tables rise only inches from the floor, and I sat with my legs folded beneath me. At first this seemed like a good idea, but after ten minutes my taste buds envied the numbness of my legs and I struggled to maintain my posture.

We had come to Japan in the summer. The flowers were blooming, the sun was blazing, and the exquisite gardens of Kyoto piqued our interest. My father and I were traveling through Asia for mission and pilgrimage purposes, but Kyoto's charm and these gracious hosts interrupted our schedule.

The fish didn't like being in my mouth. It was my prisoner of war, and I wanted to free it. The Japanese take great pride in presenting their food to foreigners, and I knew it would be offensive to reject this delicacy. But what choice did I have? My jaw was locked, my tongue was tied, and my mouth mutinied against me.

From the bowels of my being, I suddenly bellowed up the courage to swallow the thing—rice and all. It tasted of salt and shore, but after a quick breath and a short prayer, I put in my stomach what belonged in the sea and admitted to those around me that I had just lost my sushi virginity.

Sushi can be rolled up into one very fitting word: accidental. According to legend, sushi was a culinary mistake. Long before electricity and refrigerators, Oriental chefs preserved their fish with rice, salt, and stone. In the second century, a character appeared in a Chinese dictionary that meant *fish pickled with rice and salt.* This fermentation process quickly spread throughout Asia.

When the Japanese learned this technique, they modified it by sandwiching the salted fish between two stones. Several weeks later, they added a thin layer of rice to the fish until the fermentation process was complete. The rice was removed and the fish was eaten. Over time, however, the rice and fish weren't separated and the Japanese began eating them together. Sushi was suddenly born. In the eighteenth century, a clever chef named Hanaya Yohei (1799–1858) discarded the fermentation process altogether and served sushi that could be eaten on the go. It was called *nigirizushi,* and it became a fast-food dish long before fast food was popular.

A FRESHER FAITH—A SUSHI FAITH

Our culture craves raw reality. Give us reality television shows and we're glued to the screen for hours waiting to see who will be thrown off the island or disqualified from the games. We've exchanged the Partridge family for the Osbourne family because at least we know the Osbourne family is real. We are tired of scripted characters reciting perfect lines. We don't want facades. We want reality—the good, the bad, and the downright disgusting.

Our Christianity is the same. We want a faith that is as raw and fresh as sushi. No more of the blond-haired, blue-eyed Jesus who is too lofty to be relevant to lives. We are discovering afresh the real Jesus, the authentic Jesus, who, being 100 percent God, was also 100 percent man. The same hand that carved out valleys in the Old Testament cleaned Himself after a bad case of diarrhea in the New. That's the Jesus we want—a Jesus who identifies with our daily experiences; a Jesus who left his Home above to sink to earth below; a Jesus who boarded the airplane of suffering and experienced the turbulence of God's righteous wrath.

We want a Jesus with guts and grit.

Only that kind of Christ can understand our temptations. Only that kind of Christ can give us hope in the midst of our storms. Only that kind of Christ can nourish us with spiritual appetites. We want a Christ who is raw and a faith that is relevant.

AN AUTHENTIC COMMUNITY

Sushi also reflects our search for community. C. S. Lewis once said, "Friendship arises out of mere companionship when two or more of the companions discover that they have in common some insight or interest or even taste."[1] In the 1950s, boy met girl at soda fountains. Today they meet at sushi bars. According to the National Sushi Society, the number of sushi bars in the United States quintupled from 1988 to 1998 alone, and food trends expert Phil Lembert remarked, "Sushi may well be the new pizza."[2]

Why do we want community—whether at a sushi bar or a '50s malt shop? Because we burn for belonging. (Just look at a middle school cafeteria when everyone's finding a seat.) God gave us the desire for community so He alone could satisfy it.

Originally created to walk with God in the garden (Genesis 2:8), God's people maintain an upward relationship that requires time and sacrifice. Our passions are fully expressed in our relationship with God, and only when we engage the Creator can we cultivate outward relationships with others. The apostle John connects the upward and outward in this way: "But if we walk in the light, God himself being the light, we also experience a shared life with one another" (1 John 1:7). Like the 90-degree angle of a T-square, if the vertical dimension is not perpendicular, our horizontal will be misaligned as well.

Churches have much to learn from sushi bars. In 1953, Martin Luther King Jr. said, "I am [ashamed] and appalled that eleven o'clock on Sunday morning is the most segregated hour in Christian America."[3] In many areas of America this is still true. In contrast, sushi bars have become a community for the culture. It is a place that brings together people of every interest, demographic, and race. The sushi experience is gaining momentum in America and is one of the fastest ways to meet new people and make new friends. It doesn't matter who you are or where you're from; you'll always be welcome in the sushi bar.

THE HUMAN SOUL AND WORSHIP

Deep beyond this need for community with each other lies our need for community with God—a personal communion based upon worshiping the Creator. The human soul was created to worship.

Not all bow down to the Judeo-Christian God, but everyone bows down to something. We might not take a knee to idols or animals. We might not even worship in churches or shrines. But every one of us elevates something in our lives that pulls praise from our lips. Perhaps we worship football or music. Perhaps fashion or entertainment. Even atheists, who have no God to worship, elevate their intellects and idolize their rationale. The question is not *if* we are worshiping; the question is *what* we are worshiping.

While traveling through the Orient, I encountered Buddhism at its best. Since Buddhist and Shinto shrines are scattered throughout Asia, we decided to visit one. Planted deeply in the isolated hills of Japan, this monastery took several hours to reach by car. An enormous red arch greeted us at the entrance of the camp, and a tall, golden Buddha stood behind it. It must have been a hundred feet tall, glowing from the sun's reflected rays. It was the fo-

> the Buddhists' singing reflected the universal yearning for worship. it's in our blood and bones.

cal point of the entire monastic community, and quite frankly, it reminded me of the chubby Buddha sitting beside the cash register at my favorite Chinese restaurant.

After exploring the shrines, gongs, and other points of interest, I stopped to rest in Buddha's shade near a traditional Japanese building. A sound captured my attention. It was a foreign noise, a rich and novel noise. I peered into the building and saw five or six monks sitting in a row, bellowing deep, rhythmic chants. It was a continuous noise, and they scattered their breathing to maintain their sound.

Huuummmmm. Huuummmmm. Huuummmmm.

Each one took a deep breath, filling his lungs with fresh oxygen and then slowly letting it out. I tried to make that sound myself, but my voice was pitched higher and out of place. The sounds came from the deepest parts of their guts, ripe and warm, filled with the history of millions of monks who have echoed that sound before. I listened in awe.

It was very different from the kind of singing I was used to in church. Being a Baptist, I don't typically chant in church, and we Baptists certainly don't give up our pews to sit on a cold wooden floor. Our songs are linear, beginning and ending rather quickly. For the most part, we stand up to sing, and some of us raise our hands in the air. But as I listened to these monks, I encountered a different kind of song, a cyclical sound. There was no beginning or end, just the moment and the movement. And though these men were not worshiping the one true God found in the person of Jesus Christ, their singing reflected the universal yearning for worship. And it confirmed in my mind that the human soul is created to praise. It's in our blood and bones.

Music is a vital part of Christian worship. Throughout the history of the church, there have been many forms of music, from chants and canticles to folk songs and gospel hymns. Some contain biblical passages like the Psalms; others include thoughts about God and the Christian faith. God has many pipes in His organ, and He receives praise from the noises of every limb beneath the head of Christ.

CHOPSTICKS AND PRAISE SONGS

These days, new hymns are being written for the church. Contemporary Christian music and praise choruses are springing up in churches throughout the world and are being used in corporate worship. While hymns are generally sung *about* God, and praise songs are sung *to* God, we must remember that Christian music will always be changing. Its beat, rhythm, and melody may alter, but there are some things that should never be abandoned—its faithfulness to biblical doctrines, theology, and God-centeredness. These are the nonnegotiables of

Christian music and must be written in bold, permanent marker. Other elements can be sketched in pencil.

Modern chopsticks are made from many materials—bamboo, plastic, bone, jade, and ivory. It's been rumored that silver chopsticks were used in the Chinese imperial palace for the detection of poison in the emperor's meal. If the food was poisoned, the chopsticks would blacken when the poison encountered the silver. And someone usually lost his life because of it.

Christian music needs a Chinese chopstick test. Years ago, I attended a church in my city for the first time. Several friends told me that it was the hip, new church in the area, so I went to see it for myself. As I sang the praise music, I noticed a theme threaded throughout the service—the songs had nothing to do with God. Some of the tunes described the Christian life; others contained verses about struggles and temptations. Still others included a "pull yourself up by the bootstraps" message. It was a Sunday morning I'll never forget because I was struggling with a sin I couldn't get rid of. So there I stood, singing songs about how I can pull myself out of my problems while my soul was craving a worship experience that took the focus off my abilities and placed it on God's glory. Only God could lift me from my mire, and I left the sanctuary disgusted and dirty from digging in my own self-centeredness.

> when worship revolves around us, our lives are unbalanced. . . . we become spiritually schizophrenic.

Worship is giving to God what He has already given to us. We give Him our heads and hands—we know Him, love Him, and serve Him. But when worship revolves around us, our lives are unbalanced. We become a two-headed monster, praising God while at the same time applauding ourselves. We become spiritually schizophrenic, and with

Paul we confess, "Yes. I'm full of myself—after all, I've spent a long time in sin's prison. What I don't understand about myself is that I decide one way, but then I act another, doing things I absolutely despise" (Romans 7:15). When we worship ourselves, loving Jekyll becomes unholy Hyde. And we fail the Chinese chopstick test—our worship chopsticks are turning black from our self-centered poison.

MUSIC THAT WORSHIPS GOD

Music finds its primary purpose in the worship of God. I'm a sucker for all kinds of music—blues, jazz, classical, and some reggae here and there. And I love all the uses of music—entertainment, relaxation, and therapy. But music finds ultimate significance in the adoration of its creator. While the psalmist does say, "Sing God a brand-new song" (Psalm 96:1), there's nothing wrong with the old ones. Some of the greatest hymns of the faith were written when America was still in diapers—not even a nation. In 1739, Charles Wesley wrote these words:

And can it be that I should gain
An interest in the Savior's blood?
Died he for me, who caused his pain?
For me, who him to death pursued?
Amazing love! How can it be
That thou, my God, should die for me?

He left his Father's throne above,
So free, so infinite his grace;
Emptied himself of all but love,
And bled for Adam's helpless race.
'Tis mercy all, immense and free;
For, O my God it found out me.

Long my imprisoned spirit lay
Fast bound in sin and nature's night;
Thine eye diffused a quickening ray,
I woke, the dungeon flamed with light.
My chains fell off, my heart was free.
I rose, went forth, and followed thee.

No condemnation now I dread;
Jesus, and all in him is mine!
Alive in him, my living Head,
And clothed in righteousness divine.
Bold I approach the eternal throne
And claim the crown, through Christ, my own.[4]

This song packs a powerful theological punch. Wesley loaded it with spiritual truths and insights into the life we have in Jesus. Just because a hymn is old does not mean it should be discarded, for it too was once brand spanking new. On the flip side, just because a hymn is new doesn't mean it's worth singing. The quality of a song is found in its content.

Here's one of my favorite modern hymns, "In Christ Alone," written by Stuart Townsend and Keith Getty:

In Christ alone my hope is found;
He is my light, my strength, my song;
This cornerstone, this solid ground,
Firm through the fiercest drought and storm.
What heights of love, what depths of peace,
When fears are stilled, when strivings cease!

My comforter, my all in all—
Here in the love of Christ I stand.

In Christ alone, who took on flesh,
Fullness of God in helpless babe!
This gift of love and righteousness,
Scorned by the ones He came to save.
Till on that cross as Jesus died,
The wrath of God was satisfied;
For every sin on Him was laid—
Here in the death of Christ I live.

There in the ground His body lay,
Light of the world by darkness slain;
Then bursting forth in glorious day,
Up from the grave He rose again!
And as He stands in victory,
Sin's curse has lost its grip on me;
For I am His and He is mine—
Bought with the precious blood of Christ.

No guilt in life, no fear in death—
This is the power of Christ in me;
From life's first cry to final breath,
Jesus commands my destiny.
No power of hell, no scheme of man,
Can ever pluck me from His hand;
Till He returns or calls me home—
Here in the power of Christ I'll stand.[5]

This isn't miniskirt music—songs that barely cover the essentials. In this hymn Jesus Christ is the theme. His saving work on the cross is adored and His power to keep us from hell magnified. Songs like these revere the God who sits high upon His throne while mortals are kept humbly before His feet.

a God-centered life goes against our grain. we want to be on top.

But a God-centered life goes against our grain. We want to be on top. Yet throughout the history of Christianity, God has raised up individuals whose lives revolved around something greater than themselves. For Francois Fénelon, God was his ultimate fulfillment: "The more one loves God, the more one is content."[6] For John Bunyan, God was always present: "Now was God and Christ continually before my face."[7] And for Martin Luther, God was his true and only source of provision: "I have a rich Master who takes care of me while I am singing or sleeping."[8]

○ ○ ○ ○ ○ ○

They say it's the world's most deadly feast. Also known as the puffer fish, *fugu* is a type of sushi that contains lethal amounts of tetrodotoxin, a poison twelve thousand times more deadly than cyanide. Those who have been poisoned by tetrodotoxin are paralyzed and eventually die from asphyxiation. Though there is no known antidote to tetrodotoxin, the Japanese catch and consume more than ten thousand tons of fugu every year. This dish can be expensive (up to $200 at well-known restaurants) and requires a licensed and highly skilled chef to prepare it.

Japan has always fed its people from the sea. The blue waters surrounding the island nation are warmed by the *Kuroshio*, the rich, flowing current that contributes to the abundance of fish and shellfish. But if you find yourself eating fugu, be aware that, if not properly prepared, this sushi might be your last meal.

Like fugu, a human-centered life poisons us and threatens the health of our churches. The hunger of my generation for spiritual depth is growing, and revival is breaking out among youth groups and college ministries. Our generation is sick of navigating shallow creeks and empty streams. We are going deeper—submarine deep—to explore the hidden blessings that God keeps below the surface.

There are many types of sushi—finger sushi, box sushi, rolled sushi, battleship sushi,and scattered sushi. And then there's sashimi . . . the raw stuff straight from the sea. Each type has a distinct history, texture, and taste. And in an age of mega meal combos, it doesn't hurt that sushi is low in fat and cholesterol, and that each roll contains fewer than one hundred calories.

Personally, the California roll is my favorite, though the Philadelphia roll—smoked salmon, cream cheese, and cucumber—also ranks highly (my sushi palette has a long way to go). I like the California roll not only because of the cucumber, crabmeat, and avocado surrounded by a layer of rice and sesame seeds, but also because it reminds me to examine what's at the center. What does the core of my life conceal? Pride? Lust? Envy? Sushi holds me accountable in a way and prompts me to keep God at my center. I am learning to go back to the Scriptures, the raw text, to celebrate and participate in the community that Christ offers to every believer. While it's always important to read what others say about God, it's best to digest the fresh Word of God for ourselves. And when we do, we discover the center of our substance.

It's the most important decision I've had to make since 1978 when I decided to get a bikini wax.

—**ARNOLD SCHWARZENEGGER,** on running for governor of California

blue enough

BLUE — behind, beside, below me. I gasped, straining above the surface of the water. It was air I sought, but instead I swallowed a mouthful of chlorine.

I hated swimming lessons. Maybe it was the sting of icy water at seven o'clock in the morning, or perhaps the smell of sunscreen on my nose, or quite possibly the exhaustion that comes from treading water when the body is too skinny to float. Whatever the reason, I was learning to swim and drowning in the process.

From below the surface, I saw my friends on the edge of the pool. They were blurred and disfigured, waving their arms like ghosts above the twisting ripples. I felt alone and haunted, bobbing to the bottom and back, fighting in slow motion against the heaviness. My legs were sore, my lungs were hot, and the tiny breaths of oxygen I salvaged weren't enough.

It's amazing what you think about when you're drowning. I guess some people think about families and friends. Others consider unchecked e-mails, unanswered voice mails, and overdue apologies. But as I sank to the bottom of the pool, I didn't think about any of those things. The only thing on my mind was oxygen—fresh, rich, life-giving air—and I would have done anything, and I mean *anything*, to get it.

o o o o o o

On August 29, 2005, Louisiana needed oxygen. Hurricane Katrina had formed the sixth largest storm ever documented, with sustained winds of 175 miles per hour. As the storm approached New Orleans, the winds subsided to 125 miles per hour, but still they tore viciously into the city. The wind uprooted ancient oak trees and scraped against the white skull of the Superdome until the sports arena was raw with damage. For those who witnessed the storm, it was hell from above.

But it was also hell from below. Eighty percent of New Orleans lies below sea level, and the twenty-three-foot levees couldn't keep the water out. Surrounded on one side by Lake Pontchartrain and on the other by the mouth of the mighty Mississippi, most of the city quickly flooded. The storm surge also devastated the coasts of Alabama and Mississippi, making it the most destructive natural disaster in the history of the United States, not to mention the most expensive—Katrina caused more than $81 billion in damage.

Several weeks after Katrina struck, all fifty states had provided shelter for evacuees, and many educational institutions had opened their doors to 100,000 displaced college and university students. Over seventy countries provided money and assistance, including Sri Lanka, a nation still recovering from its own tsunami in December 2004. But for those who had lost jobs, homes, and family in the storm, the future was going to be grim.

Many people questioned the goodness of God. How could an all-powerful, loving God let this happen? Was He on the phone? Fast asleep? In a straightjacket? Some considered the hurricane to be a judgment on the city because of its notorious immorality. Others wondered why the churches in the area sustained more damage than, say, the bars of Bourbon Street.

WHERE THE BLUES WERE BORN

A year before Katrina struck, Rebecca and I visited New Orleans. Since her home is New Orleans, we often strolled the city together. We visited her old stomping grounds—her high school, her church, and her favorite restaurants. We walked down St. Charles Avenue, shopped in the French Quarter, and ate beignets at Café du Monde. But my favorite place in New Orleans was a hole-in-the-wall jazz club called Preservation Hall.

Born in 1961, Preservation Hall features some of the greatest jazz musicians in New Orleans. The weathered exterior of the building dates back to the 1800s, and not much has changed since then. There's no air conditioning, yet despite the heat, people wait in long lines every night to experience jazz, the music America made. At times they play the old stuff like Glenn Miller, Benny Goodman, and big band music. But the first time I entered the musky room, I found the wait was worth the while and I was greeted not with jazz, or big band, or even ragtime, but with blues. And not just any kind of blues, but deep, earthy, midnight blues, a shade that could pass for purple were it in the right light.

The blues were born in dark places. Places like Southern plantations where African slaves toiled beneath the burning sun. Frederick Douglass, a slave who escaped at the age of twenty-one, wrote that the slaves living on his old plantation would "make the dense old woods, for miles around, reverberate with their wild notes. . . . There was ever a tinge of deep melancholy."[1] Throughout the fields of Alabama, Mississippi, and Georgia, "whooping" or "cotton field hollers" could be heard. These were the laments of slaves who were working for their masters, songs not set to words but moans and groans from the deepest part of the soul. Some were sharp, others short. Some wavered, others swooped. But most were slow and mournful, pulsing with memories of their families back in Africa.

Eventually, English words were wrapped around these tunes. In between hits of railroad hammers, lines of music were sung. The beat for their music had already been determined by their work, and they filled in the rest. The songs were also songs for practical uses. When a slave needed a drink of water, for example, he or she would sing the "Water Call":

> Bring me a little water, Silvie,
> Bring me a little water now.
> Bring me a little water, Silvie,
> Every little once in a while.[2]

Slaves on old plantations soon absorbed European music like Wesleyan hymns, Irish fiddle tunes, and ballads, yet they wrapped them around the struggles of slavery and made them their own. In the 1870s and '80s, the blues traveled from the field where they were born to the city where they were sold. Throughout the Southern states the blues could be heard, especially around the Mississippi River. Pianist Jelly Roll Morton described a blues singer living in New Orleans in 1902:

The one blues I never can forget . . . happened to be played by a woman that lived next door to my godmother's in the Garden District. The name of this musician was Mamie Desdoumes. Two middle fingers of her right hand had been cut off, so she played the blues with only three fingers on her right hand. She only knew this one tune and she played it all day long after she would first get up in the morning:

I stood on the corner, my feet was dripping wet,
I asked every man I met . . .
Can't give me a dollar, give me a lousy dime,
Just to feed that hungry man of mine.[3]

As the blues traveled to different parts of the Unites States during the twentieth century, it became more urban and transitioned from the vocal/guitar to the slick delivery of electronics, brass, and woodwinds.[4] Though its location changed, the spirit of the blues remained the same. Austin Sonnier Jr. explained, "The blues is not merely a marriage of words and music. Its lyrics tell one story and its music tells another. It

> God has not forgotten the city that He scooped out of the Louisiana swamps.

penetrates deeply into the soul and pulls out what does not belong there, replacing it with what does."[5]

How can this genre of music have such an effect on its listeners? Besides improvisation and varied melodic lines, the blues include "blue notes" that are sprinkled throughout the tune. Blue notes are commonly located on the third, fifth, and seventh degrees of a scale and provide a sense of tension for the listener.[6]

On August 29, 2005, New Orleans hit a very blue note. The waters that spilled into the city would remain there for weeks, creating an environment of disease, famine, and death. Bodies were seen floating down the streets, severely decomposed and bloated. The total death count rose to 1,836 souls.

Approximately eighty years before Katrina, Dr. R. G. Lee, pastor of First Baptist Church of New Orleans, preached a sermon called "The Roses Will Bloom Again." It was a sermon of hope and comfort, a sermon that promised triumphs after trials and rainbows after rainstorms. It was a sermon born in the blues and preached in the wake of World War I when the optimism of humanity was shattered by the realism of depravity.

"The disciples thought the roses would never bloom again," Pastor Lee said, "when they knew that Jesus was in the grave. But the roses did bloom! And after the stress, after the stress and storm, the roses bloomed. After the storm, the sun shone. And after the night, the dawn. And after the trial, the glory . . . the roses bloom again!"[7]

As the city of New Orleans rebuilds, these prophetic words, preached nearly a century ago, continue to offer hope. Hope that one day new trees will be planted, new restaurants will be opened, and churches will continue to glow in a morally dark land. God has not forgotten the city that He scooped out of the Louisiana swamps, and though Dr. Lee died in 1978, his words remind us that roses aren't without thorns and pain is not without purpose. The Crescent City will smile once more. And the roses will bloom again.

A new day dawned when I became an art major in college. My high school friends had scattered across the country, my braces had finally been torn from my teeth, and I was ready to grab life by the horns. Little did I know that horns were easier to paint than grab. Fraternities and marching bands weren't my thing (though I play a killer kazoo), but art had always attracted me, so I chose it as a major.

In kindergarten I painted with careless fingers—clumsy and chaotic, throwing paint across the frightened canvas. They were the fingers of a five-year-old that hadn't yet mastered the art of moderation. I hated coloring books. The lines felt confining, too restricting and determined. I was the kid who colored outside the lines, saw life outside the box, and even was scolded by a teacher for trying to paint the easel instead of the paper.

ART AND THE FACE OF CHRIST

Throughout my childhood, I traveled the world with my father. I saw art of unequalled magnitude, works of great masters like van Gogh and Michelangelo. The more I studied their styles, the more I sought their secrets. By my early teens I had seen the sculptures in Florence, the paintings in Rome, and the illuminated Celtic manuscripts in Ireland. I strolled through galleries and museums, observed sidewalk art and photo-realistic portraits.

> God could have chosen to be abstract and absent. but He chose another way . . . and made Himself accessible to everyone.

But one painting in particular made an impression on me above all others—the *Mona Lisa.* It was a small painting, overhyped and not at all what I had imagined. But there was something about her grin that grabbed my gaze. Why was she smiling like that? Did she know something I didn't? Did she see something I couldn't? How eerie her smile must have been to the thief who stole her in 1911 from the Salon Carré in the Louvre. Some art historians say that that *Mona Lisa* was a self-portrait of Leonardo da Vinci because when his profile is superimposed over hers, the contours line up exactly. Was this the secret of her smile? Perhaps. No one really knows. Whatever the case, the *Mona*

Lisa brewed in my brain for years.

God smiles at us through the face of Christ. Jesus reminded His disciples, "To see me is to see the Father" (John 14:9). The eyes that introduced seas to shores came down to earth to look upon us up close. No longer did God use a microscope; He became a specimen. God could have chosen to be abstract and absent. But He chose another way, a painful way. And God Wal-Marted Himself in the person of Jesus Christ and made Himself accessible to everyone.

BLUE APRIL

I met April in my first year of college. She didn't run in my circles or go to my school, but her bright blue hair caught my eye, and we became friends. April's life matched the color of her hair. Her parents divorced because her father was abusive, and her current boyfriend wasn't much better. "If I go to heaven," she told me, "I'm going to ask God where He was when my father beat me up. Why would an all-powerful God let that happen to me?"

> it took us back to those careless summer days when frying ants beneath a magnifying glass was the thing to do.

I had no easy answers. In fact, they didn't even exist. But every Thursday a group of my friends and I went swing dancing with blue-haired April, and afterward we caught some midnight sushi and talked about God. Swing dancing and sushi had a way of resetting the brain. No matter how much life hurt, every Thursday it got better.

Maybe it was the tempo, or perhaps the racing rhythm, but when we met at the swing club, time slowed down. It was like we were living in an era of long ago, when swing kids danced in the face of war and Americans came together to fight against a common enemy. It took us back to those careless summer days when frying ants beneath a magnifying glass was the thing to do. When four feet of water was the deep end of the swimming pool and the diving board towered over the depths. Swing dancing was a coping mechanism for the troubles that come from being human.

Karl Marx once said that religion is just a crutch for the weak. Perhaps he was right. But Christ is way more than just our crutch. He's our very life support. He gives oxygen to the suffocating and blood to the anemic. He's the cardiologist who gives us hearts of flesh and the neurologist who gives us minds of Christ. Without His love, we would drown in selfishness. Without His grace, we would feel the white-hot heat of God's wrath against us. Without Him, we're ice for the blender. Perhaps Karl Marx is right and we do have a coping mechanism, but it's better to limp with God to heaven than to leap to hell without Him.

BLUE PHOBIA

Painting came as a pleasure to me. For hours, I crafted portraits in my college's art studio. With my ruler I deconstructed the mathematics of vanishing points and linear horizons, paying special attention to proportions and spatial relationships. I spent hours examining the contours of the face, noticing the way the chin drops gently beneath the cheeks, the way light licks everyone a little differently, bending around bones and struggling around shadows. For months I mixed yellows with greens, oranges with browns, reds with purples. I discovered colors I'd never known about—sage, chartreuse, and fuchsia. I swirled lights with darks and noticed how each pigment plays a special role in the process of a painting. No color escaped my attention. Well, except one.

Blue. It had always evaded me. It didn't matter what I was painting—a waterfall, an ocean, or a book—if it needed to be blue, it was going to be bad. Maybe it was blue's tendency to become green when yellow came too close. Maybe it was the frustration of never really being able to capture the color of the sky. Blue disappointed and perplexed me. Even when I painted the darkness—thunderclouds torn by jagged lightning and winds—the blues always looked shallow and misty. Before long I had developed a bad case of blue phobia and avoided the color at all cost.

I avoided it not just in my art, but also in my life. I hated the blue notes of my life—the hospitals and the heartaches. When my Acura needed a new engine, I asked God what I had done to make Him so angry. When my body couldn't handle the daily dose of steroids to treat my digestive disease, I questioned God's goodness. I couldn't understand blue. But I soon realized that God was using the blue notes to highlight the high notes. He took me through the mud so I would appreciate the shower, and I was refreshed by the cleansing words of the Bible.

THE VALLEY OF VISION

God doesn't promise a life without problems or pain. He doesn't always lead us by streams of quiet water. Sometimes He takes us through the valley so we can appreciate His presence. This Puritan prayer called "The Valley of Vision" captures the essence of Christian suffering:

> Lord, high and holy, meek and lowly,
> Thou hast brought me to the valley of vision,
> where I live in the depths but see thee in the heights;
> hemmed in by mountains of sin I behold thy glory.

Let me learn by paradox

that the way down is the way up,

that to be low is to be high,

that the broken heart is the healed heart,

that the contrite spirit is the rejoicing spirit,

that the repenting soul is the victorious soul,

that to have nothing is to possess all,

that to bear the cross is to wear the crown,

that to give is to receive,

that the valley is the place of vision.

Lord, in the daytime stars can be seen from deepest wells,

and the deeper the wells the brighter thy stars shine;

Let me find thy light in my darkness,

thy life in my death,

thy joy in my sorrow,

thy grace in my sin,

thy riches in my poverty,

thy glory in my valley.[8]

Only in the midnight moments, the jazzy hell moments, do our eyes fully see the light of the Lord. Suffering corrects our posture and aids our gaze. When life is easy and troubles few, we stand tall and think well of ourselves. But such a stance is gnarled before the God of grace and glory. Being broken is to heal. And the bottom of the bucket raises our heads to the One who "reached down from on high and took hold of me" (Psalm 18:16 NIV). Even the sun has dark spots, but Jesus is unaffected by the acne of imperfections. And He sustains us through the storm.

PLAYING THE BLUES WITH US

Christ is not a classical conductor, standing above the band to direct our tempo and guide our melody. Rather, He's playing the blues with us. Like a jazz band leader, He's one of the members. The Bible says, "When the time came, he set aside the privileges of deity and took on the status of a slave, became human! Having become human, he stayed human. It was an incredibly humbling process" (Philippians 2:8). We're told He was tempted in every way that we are tempted (Hebrews 4:15). The air we breathe, He breathed; the tune we hum, He hummed; and the beat we keep, He kept. His song was harder to play than ours, but He never missed a note.

I don't paint much anymore. I suppose words have become my pigment and computer screens my canvas. But every once in a while I'll pick up a paintbrush and remind myself of days gone by, days of endless drawings on dusty college easels. Days of Doritos for breakfast and sushi for dinner. Days of blue-haired April and swing dancing.

Humans are born in a storm. We're surrounded by tempests of temptation and death. The waters of the world rise above our heads and we scream with the psalmist, "God, God, save me! I'm in over my head, quicksand under me, swamp water over me; I'm going down for the third time" (Psalm 69:1–2). But even in the hurricane, there are holy hushes. God whispers to us, "When you're in over your head, I'll be there with you. When you're in rough waters, you will not go down" (Isaiah 43:2). Even the mighty waters are subject to divine discipline. "God thunders across the waters" (Psalm 29:3); He gathers them into jars (Psalm 33:7), and at His rebuke the waters flee (Psalm 104:7).

○ ○ ○ ○ ○ ○

As I was fighting for my life beneath the surface of the water, my sister Alyce screamed for the lifeguard to save me. A forceful arm grabbed my tiny chest and pulled me to safety. It was a blurry but beautiful moment, a moment of dizzy relief. I often go to that moment when my faith grows cold and numb. When my passion for God tingles away and apathy absorbs my spiritual life. I go there when grace sounds as plain and ordinary as microwavable food waiting to be zapped.

In those blue times, I remember the blurry times, the drowning times, the bitter times, and I jump again into the waves. I inhale the water into my lungs, taste the chlorine in my mouth, and feel the cold rush of death against my ribs. And I gasp for God as though He were as healing to me as a needed breath of air. R. G. Lee once preached,

> Sometimes in the storm, when the storm is on, and the thunder crashes, the sky is inky black, danger and fear and death, it seems, ride the clouds. Not a bird to be seen or heard, only that thunder and lightning. But when the morning dawned, the earth was wonderful. Its air was fresh and washed, and the grass and leaves and flowers were clean and greener than ever, since God washed the world.[9]

And we hang on to the hope that the roses will bloom again.

One thing vampire children have to be taught early on is,
don't run with wooden stakes.

—JACK HANDEY

a
gory
gospel

KIDNEY STONES come in all shapes and sizes. Some are large, others small. Some are thin, others fat. Some are hooked and sharp, others rough and round. And yet, no matter what the shape or size, passing a kidney stone is like having a baby, only through a straw.

As several stones made their way through my body, I finally understood what C. S. Lewis meant when he said, "God whispers to us in our pleasures, speaks in our conscience, but shouts in our pain."[1] Curled up in the passenger seat of our Honda CR-V, I considered giving God a throat lozenge.

The hospital was miles away, and the green lights lingered red. The highway traffic was building, my body temperature was rising, and each second that passed brought me closer to a threshold of pain I never knew existed.

When we finally arrived, I joined a waiting room filled with broken arms, sprained ankles, and respiratory infections. Everyone was moaning about something, and those who weren't coughing shielded their children from those who were. Stumbling to the front desk, I attempted to write my name on the sign-in sheet. It should have been an easy task, but the pain shooting through my lower back dulled my skills. I resorted to scribbling like a second grader.

"Christi Gore?" the nurse asked with a smirk.

"It's Christian George." I groaned. "Pain medicine . . . kidney stone!"

I don't remember her face, but I knew she was skeptical about my illness. Later I would discover that many people feign illness at this hospital to get a pain killer fix.

"Look, I'm passing kidney stones, and they're killing me!"

"Just have a seat over there," she said, pointing to a room packed with people.

She doesn't believe me!

My wife had not yet arrived in the waiting room, and I sat with my head in my lap, suffering in my seat as a Jerry Springer rerun echoed in the distance. "Jerry! Jerry! Jerry!" A fight broke out between someone's sister and the husband she slept with. Meanwhile, the woman beside me was wheezing—and before long the gurgle in her lungs manifested itself on the ground by my foot.

Closing my eyes, I concentrated on the pain. I tried a number of remedies—rubbing my temples in circular motions, swaying from side to side, even pinching my legs to divert the pain. But it was as helpful as a Band-Aid on a broken back. I huddled in the chair and waited for my name to be called.

No more waiting, I told myself. I shuffled to the counter.

"I said take a seat, young man!" the nurse said with attitude. The authority in her voice was persuasive, but not as persuasive as the blade in my back.

"But you don't understand. I can't take the pain anymore!" Clearly causing a commotion, I turned around as a security guard approached me. His gun was gray and loaded.

But then the nurse said, "All right, come in here." She motioned the guard away. After taking my vital signs, she told me to sit tight until she returned. But it didn't matter anymore. The agony increased, my eyes rolled back, and I collapsed to the ground.

> abstract ideas on grief mean nothing when you're passing a kidney stone the size of Montana.

The next thing I remember was waking up in a secluded room, humming songs like "Jesus Loves Me" and "He's Got the Whole World in His Hands." I hadn't sung those tunes in ten years, but I remembered them as if it were Sunday school again. *Does Jesus really love me? If so, why did I have to endure this torture? If God has the whole world in His hands, why can't He scoop my suffering out of it?*

Oh, I had some pretty good answers—you can't graduate from seminary without memorizing a few of them. But all of them faded away as I lay on my back with an IV in my arm. Abstract ideas on grief mean nothing when you're passing a kidney stone the size of Montana. Everything disappears in that kind of pain—reason, theories, insights. Kidney stones actually are fairly small, only a pebble's size, but they're so painful that they can reduce the hardest criminal to a baby crying in his crib.

The next four hours weren't pleasant—catheters, blood tests, and urine samples. The morphine dulled the agony, and with my wife by my side I began reflecting on the situation. I thought about the woman in the waiting room and her hellish hack. I thought about those in developing nations who do not have access to adequate health care. I thought about that age-old problem of pain. But above all, I thought about the God who allows suffering to exist.

When I was a freshman in college, I was diagnosed with a disease called ulcerative colitis. It's a digestive disorder that results in bleeding ulcers in the colon, and the side effects of the medicine (like kidney stones, it turns out) are sometimes worse than the illness. Over the years, blood became a brother to me. Every morning I set my alarm clock two hours early so I could bleed before going to class. Twenty, sometimes thirty times a day, I suffered with God in the bathroom. I was hospitalized twice in two months. I lost a substantial amount of weight, had to take medicine to counter the effects of the steroids, and at the end of each day the pain was so great that sometimes I just wanted to give up.

Sure, I sang, "Why should I be discouraged, why should the shadows come, why should my heart feel lonely and long for heaven and home; when Jesus is my portion? My constant friend is He: His eye is on the sparrow and I know He watches me."[2] But many nights I didn't feel as if God were watching me, and when the doctor recommended major digestive surgery, I questioned the faith I had always held so close.

Suffering must be experienced before it can be explained. A chapter on suffering must emerge not from the clouds of ivory towers, but from the dark places—the hospitals, the funeral homes, and the valleys of the shadow of death. For six years I suffered with God in the bathroom, bleeding for months and years at a time. Little did I know that God was forging within me a faith that loved the Christ who bled on my behalf.

DRACULA COUNTRY

Mountains blurred past my window. Not just any mountains—Transylvanian mountains. My father and I were traveling through Romania to visit friends and encourage the seminary in Oradea, but deep down I wanted to see vampires. We were in the heart of Dracula country, and having packed my only turtleneck, I was ready for an attack.

The legend of Count Dracula finds its origin in the middle of the fifteenth century. In the winter of 1431, Vlad III was born in the German fortified town of Schassburg (now Sighisoara, Romania). His father, Vlad II of the Basarab family, had been inducted into a semi-military religious society in Nürnberg called "The Order of the Dragon." The group existed to defend Catholicism against the invading Turks, and every Friday its members wore dark costumes with the insignia of a dragon. According to experts, "The insignia consisted of a prostrate dragon, wings expanded, hanging on a cross, with its tail curled around the head."[3] Vlad III inherited the name Dracula, which means "son of the devil" in Romanian. It was a title he would certainly live up to.

When he was only a boy, Dracula and his brother were given by their father to the enemy Turks because of a war treaty. His father wrote, "Please understand that I have allowed my little children to be butchered for the sake of Christian peace."[4] Dracula was kept at the fortress of Egrigoz ("crooked eyes," in Turkish), surrounded by oak and pine trees. During his four-year captivity, his life was threatened, he lived in a constant state of fear, and he witnessed torturous acts of cruelty and terror. No doubt those experiences hardened his heart.

After he was released from prison, Dracula soon rose to power, and he used his authority mercilessly. Somewhat pale in complexion, Dracula's jet-black hair and mustache contributed to his cold and sadistic aura. He became known as Vlad the Impaler because he loved staking bodies onto spikes, his favorite torture technique. His acts of cruelty grew, as did his thirst for blood. He enjoyed skinning, boiling, decapitating, blinding, strangling, and roasting his enemies. When Dracula became ruler, he declared a law in his own country that any crime was punishable by impalement, even lying and stealing.

As far as monsters go, Dracula was as merciless as any. But he was also a gentleman. He familiarized himself with swimming, fencing, court etiquette, and horsemanship. He excelled in Latin, Slavonic, Italian, French, and Hungarian, not to mention his own Romanian tongue. He managed to hold good relations with Franciscan and Cistercian monks and built five monasteries. When he secured the throne in 1456, Dracula was a wily politician, even humorous at times, who sought to be feared rather than loved.

After a long drive through the Carpathian Mountains near Oradea, we entered a large cave filled with bats. It was dark and cold but there was enough light for me to see the stalagmites on the floor reaching up to touch the stalactites on the ceiling. Their dripping was eerie, but I inquired about the phenomenon. When mineralized water, mainly calcium carbonate, trickles from cavities in the ceiling of a cave, thin rings of calcite build upon one another, our guide explained. These rings eventually form a hollow tube that spans the height of the cave (stalactites also form on ceilings where there is a leakage of limestone and other minerals).

Sliding my hand across a slippery rock, my thoughts turned upward. I thought about grace. Perhaps humans are the recipients of divine dripping. Indeed, faith often forms like a stalagmite. The apostle John wrote, "This is the kind of love we are talking about—not that we once upon a time loved God, but that he loved us" (1 John 4:10). In the blackness of time, God dripped His love onto us, creating us, forming us, and shaping us. God connects us to Himself one drip at a time. It's not our dripping that elevates us; gravity won't allow that. But in His grace, God bends down to us and brings us to a place of contact. We touch the One who touches us and we confess with the psalmist, "He made creeks flow out from sheer rock, and water pour out like a river" (Psalm 78:16).

Over a thousand years before Count Dracula lived, Jesus Christ was impaled to a wooden stake. The Romans had mastered the technique, nailing their subjects to wood. According to Pierre Barbet, a physician who crucified cadavers in a medical experiment, the Roman nails probably were driven into Christ's wrists, not His hands. This would have severed His median nerves and caused unequaled pain. "Christ must then have agonized and died and have become fixed in a cadaverous rigidity, with the thumbs bent inward into his palms."[5] For the Jewish faith, no

> suffering is the reality of our mortality. not just physical pain, but emotional and spiritual pain. no one escapes it.

punishment was worse. It is written, "Anyone who is hung on a tree is under God's curse" (Deuteronomy 21:23 NIV).

Jesus could have called ten thousand angels to help Him down from that cross (see Matthew 26:53). A little word would have done it. Perhaps even a passing glance and a legion of samurai seraphim would have hacked through the Roman army to save the Savior. They would have comforted Him as they did in the wilderness after He dueled with the Devil (Matthew 4). But no word was ever uttered, except "Father, forgive them; they don't know what they're doing" (Luke 23:34). And with every strike of the hammer, God was dripping us closer to Himself. With every sting of the whip, God was drawing us to His side.

A faith that doesn't cost much isn't worth much. Christians are called to take up our crosses and follow God. Our crosses aren't made of Styrofoam, but neither are they made of iron. The wood is enough for us, and we can carry them, knowing they have been carried before.

Suffering is the reality of our mortality. Not just physical pain, but emotional and spiritual pain scars our bodies. No one escapes it. Not the rich or the beautiful. Not the successful or the talented. Painkillers can't soothe it and prescriptions can't cure it. Ever since Adam and Eve ate the forbidden fruit, death, murder, and selfishness were introduced into the world. Animals ate one another, residents of continents crushed one another, and suffering flexed its thorny muscle.

THE PARADIGM OF PAIN

Every child understands the universal paradigm of pain. From the sting of a bee to the stub of a toe, we quickly learn the boundaries that are set for us. The older we get, however, the more we medicate ourselves at the first thought of pain. Have a headache? Pop a pill. Tummy ache? Take a Tums. And while medical advances have performed miracles of hope for many throughout the world, we have conditioned ourselves to think of suffering as always negative and healing as always positive. But God forges His servants on the anvil of affliction. We must never seek suffering in a masochistic way, but we must agree with Paul that it produces perseverance, character, and, eventually, hope (Romans 5:3–4).

It has become popular in our culture to view every kind of suffering as God's judgment on our lives. While there are biblical examples of those whose sin caused great tragedy,[6] the Bible teaches that God allows suffering to bring His children to Himself. Suffering chisels away our imperfections and creates within us a desire for ultimate healing.

We often suffer from never having suffered.

Only after losing family, friends, and health does Job finally come to understand the sovereignty of God. Only after the psalmist said, "It was good for me to be afflicted so that I might learn your decrees" (Psalm 119:71 NIV), did he continue to love the law of the Lord. When Paul asked to have his thorn removed from his flesh, God said no. When Peter asked about his future, Jesus predicted martyrdom. In fact, many of the Christians in the early Roman era were murdered because of their faith. They were beaten with sticks and impaled to crosses. For them, life was a battlefield, not a playground, and the worship of God was their ultimate agenda, even in the face of affliction.

My generation is a product of broken homes and broken hearts. We are a generation with real questions, and we won't settle for artificial answers. We have learned to grab God wherever we can get Him. We are advancing in the promotion of biblical principles, social justice, and mission work. But we're also saturated with suffering. Most of my closest friends grew up in fractured homes. Pornography, food addictions, and depression assail us on every level.

> God became a baby to suffer with and for us—the Judge became the judged.

In the midst of our suffering, we are asking tough questions and are discovering that God is full of answers. He suffers with us and ultimately brings true healing to our fragile lives.

I still remember the pain of those kidney stones. There's no pain in the world like it—a pain to make even Count Dracula squirm. And yet it brings us comfort knowing that Christ endured pain far beyond the pain of kidney stones. In his book *Virtual Faith*, Tom Beaudoin suggested that the baby boomer generation has been very quick to gloss over the crucifixion of Christ and go straight to the victory and hope of the resurrection. The younger generations, however, are slowing down and reexamining the suffering of Christ.[7] My generation wants to study the reality of the brutality. We want to take a closer look at those nails that split His tendons. And by examining the suffering of Christ, we discover how we are comforted in ours.

God became a baby to suffer with and for us—the Judge became the judged.[8] He didn't have to do this. He could have easily abandoned earth after we sinned. He could have chosen another planet on which to accomplish His will. But with arms wide open He embraced the nails, the beatings, and the bruises. For our sake He "knew pain firsthand" (Isaiah 53:3). Like a sponge, He absorbed the wrath that our sins provoked. And in the middle of His storm, when the sun had to look the other way, Jesus cried out, "My God, my God, why have you abandoned me?" (Matthew 27:46).

In 586 B.C., the Babylonians took God's people into captivity. It was a time of great suffering and anguish for the Israelites, and to make matters worse, the Babylonians taunted them. "Our captors asked us for songs, our tormentors demanded songs of joy; they said, 'Sing us one of the songs of Zion!'" (Psalm 137:3 NIV). Instead of singing, the Israelites hung their harps on the willow trees.

But we as Christians can pick up our harps and sing despite our storms. We can finish the hymn "I sing because I'm happy, I sing because I'm free; for His eye is on the sparrow, and I know he watches me."[9] We sing because we know that storms aren't forever and one day mourning will turn to morning. We sing because we worship the God who will not give us more than we can bear. He squeezes us in order to shape us. He breaks us in order to build us. And soon we discover that in our brokenness, God Himself is singing with us, suffering beside us, and holding us up when all the world would tear us down.

As we exited the Romanian cave, I felt a sting of disappointment. While the bats were certainly cool, I still wanted to gaze at the burning eyes of a vampire. In Romanian folklore, bats are believed to be embodiments of evil spirits. The Romanian bat is smaller than its South American counterpart, but it is still considered dangerous by peasants throughout the country. According to myth expert Raymond McNally, "[Peasants] relate strange tales of people with bat wounds becoming demented and wishing to bite others."[10] But I didn't meet any of those people, and the closest thing I got to a bat bite was the rash I developed from the turtleneck.

> the gospel of Jesus Christ *is* a gory gospel. it's an R-rated gospel... there was no anesthesia for Christ's agony.

Unlike Count Dracula who took blood, Jesus Christ offered His blood. He extended His neck to us that we might partake in His fellowship. We are His mosquitoes, feeding on Him for life. Every time Christians gather for Holy Communion, we think of Christ's words to His disciples, "This is my blood, God's new covenant, poured out for many people" (Mark 14:24).

Sometimes I'll be flipping through the channels on my television and I'll come across a surgery being performed. If I'm eating dinner, I'll keep flipping for fear of losing my appetite, but every once in a while I'll get the guts to watch the entirety. I get queasy as the knife slices through layers of skin and the suction tube fills with fluid. I have to look away when they saw through bones and stitch up blood vessels. And I feel sorry for the patient, even though I know that the poor guy getting his eyeball cut up doesn't feel a thing.

The gospel of Jesus Christ *is* a gory gospel. It's an R-rated gospel, a blood-squirting gospel. There was no anesthesia for Christ's agony. This was the very reason He came to earth, and He wanted to be fully sensitive and alert to the divine transaction. The Christian faith is not for the fainthearted. Sometimes we want to polish the cross and smooth out the splinters, but it took a gory gospel to wash away our dirty stains.

Who is Jesus? Is He just a Jewish carpenter who was nailed to a piece of wood? Is He just a local magician casting His spells over nature? Is He just a good teacher who taught His disciples the difference between right and wrong, good and bad, life and death?

There once was a woman who had suffered through a bleeding disorder for twelve years (Luke 8:43–48). According to Leviticus 15, her constant bleeding rendered her ceremonially unclean. That means she had not been to church in 624 weeks. She hadn't slept with a man in well over a decade. She couldn't even go shopping with her girlfriends because society considered her an outcast. There was no BlueCross BlueShield for this girl, no Band-Aid to bind her wound, and no tampon to hide her blood. All the pills and prescriptions and potions couldn't prevent her pain. She was a nobody. The crowds thought so, the disciples thought so, and even she herself knew it to be true.

But Jesus said, "Somebody touched Me."

"But Lord," Simon Peter interrupted, "everybody's touching You!"

"No, Simon," Jesus said, "somebody touched Me." Jesus called a nobody a somebody.

The woman had a superstitious faith. In that day it was thought that healing came from touching. We see this tradition in Acts 19 when people came in contact with the handkerchiefs and the aprons of the apostles. It was a faith that foreshadowed a medieval European era when pilgrims traveled for miles to touch icons and relics. We even see it today on television. "Send us twenty dollars, and we'll send you a prayer handkerchief that guarantees your instant healing." Superstition!

Nevertheless, Jesus Christ accommodates Himself to her fragile, faulty, superstitious faith, and she whispers to herself, "At last, here is a man who can heal me. I know I am unclean and unworthy, but if I can just snatch His sleeve I know I will be healed." Suddenly, a nobody reaches out of nowhere and touches the hem of the garment of God. Twelve long years of bleeding stops in a heartbeat, and Jesus says, "Daughter, your faith has healed you. Go in peace." This is the only place in the New Testament where Jesus calls a woman "daughter." She goes from being a nobody, to being a somebody, to being a child of God.

Who is Jesus? He's the Great Physician who walks with us on the road to recovery and redemption.

○ ○ ○ ○ ○ ○

In 2006, a new medicine called Remicade was released in the United States for the treatment of ulcerative colitis—my incurable bleeding disorder. Researchers report that Remicade doesn't contribute to the formation of kidney stones, and thus far it has put my colitis into remission. But I still remember those dark days, those red days, those midnight moments when I longed to reach out my hand and grasp the healing garment of God. But even in the darkness, beauty was there. Looking back on my experiences, I can see how suffering was a tool in God's work shed. He used it to make me serious about my Christian convictions. And it brought me great comfort to know that Jesus, too, suffered from a bleeding disorder in the garden of Gethsemane when drops of sweat became great drops of blood (Luke 22:44).

In Romania today, there is a rumor that Count Dracula will come again to restore the country of Romania as he did in the fifteenth century. "Here, in times of stress, the peasants feel that the spirit of Dracula will be born again, or to put it more accurately, that he never really died; he is just 'undead.'"[11] While there is documented evidence that

Vlad the Impaler was assassinated in a battle near Bucharest,[12] many travel through Transylvania looking in caves and castles for his evil presence.

After Jesus had been in the tomb for three days, the Father said, "My child, get up." He declared, "My son, it's time to get on up out of that grave!" And Jesus was raised to life, and death was laid to rest. And the light of the world surfaced on the horizon, blinding vampires, demons, and darkness. That's why we sing, "What can wash away my sin? Nothing but the blood of Jesus. What can make me whole again? Nothing but the blood of Jesus. Oh! precious is that flow that makes me white as snow; no other fount I know, nothing but the blood of Jesus."[13] That's why we place all our eggs in the Easter basket.

It's a gory gospel, but it has a great ending. And a day is coming when every tear will be wiped from every eye and every sickness from every saint. And we will hold not only the hem of the garment of God, but with hands outstretched we will be embraced by the everlasting arms of the Almighty.

"They couldn't hit an elephant at this dist—"

—the last words of General John Sedgwick before taking a bullet in the face in the Battle of the Wilderness[1]

good
hamster
fluffy

HE WAS A GOOD hamster, as far as hamsters go. His name was Fluffy, and he didn't require too much. When he needed to be fed, he ate. When he needed to be walked, he scrambled along. Sometimes I came home from first grade just to watch him run around his wheel. He liked carrots, celery, and cucumber sticks, but most of all he enjoyed a good belly rub in the morning. And at night before he closed his eyes, I was there to make sure all was right and wonderful in his little hamster world.

I was a good kid, as far as kids go. I never cheated on my homework or rebelled against my parents. For some reason I cussed like a sailor in sixth grade, but that wore off in middle school. My grades were not exceptional, but they didn't scrape the bottom either. I loved animals; not just hamsters, but anything that was four-legged and furry—dogs, cats, and mice. If God made them, I wanted to know about them. And before long we had a zoo living at our house.

Summertime in Birmingham, Alabama, can make you wish God had never created the sun. Melting ice cream and burning pavement characterized the Junes, Julys, and Augusts of my youth. I have scalding hot memories from those days, memories of chlorinated kiddy pools and watermelons that had to be eaten with the whole face. One hot August day, my friends and I were playing outside my house in the sprinkler. Some of us were running through it; others were running from it. But all of us were enjoying the cool bursts of water after a long blazing day.

I thought of Fluffy and went inside our garage to see if he needed some water. His water bottle was bone dry, and I filled it.

But then I had an idea. It wasn't brilliant, but I basked in its construction. Picking up a bucket, I walked around the house to where my friends were playing. "Fluffy, maybe this will cool you off," I said, filling the bucket with water. Bits of grass mingled with the swirling water that sprayed my arms and legs. The hamster was hot in my hand as I held him over the water.

Fluffy was nervous about the idea. His heart raced and his head flinched as he avoided the rippled sunlight. But when he hit the water, his legs kicked circles beneath his body. "You're a really good swimmer," I said, watching him spring from side to side. The water was not high enough for him to reach the rim of the bucket, and I left him alone to splash around in the waves. "I'll be back in a few minutes to check on you," I said, running over to play with my friends. Five minutes turned to ten, ten to fifteen, and when I finally returned Fluffy was exhausted from paddling.

But I wasn't done with Fluffy. I wanted to see him swim longer in the bucket, so I held him there. I made sure his nose stayed above the surface, but sometimes bubbles emerged. After several minutes of this, I wanted to know how long Fluffy could hold his breath. My best record was forty-five seconds, and I wanted to see if my hamster could match it. As I held him under the water, I could feel him kicking against his liquid environment. But then the squirming slowly stopped. Floating in the middle of the bucket, Fluffy's legs were stiff and still. No longer was he splashing or moving, and as I transported him from the bucket to the grass, I realized that his chest wasn't rising like it used to. His body was cold and slimy against my skin.

I had never touched death before. Sure, I had seen it on television and read about it in comic books, but as I held my hamster in my hand I knew that I had killed it. I had committed hamster slaughter. I lied to my parents and told them that Fluffy died during the night, but I knew the truth. I knew that Fluffy was at my mercy, and on a hot summer day I gave him none.

> we humans are born with venom in our veins, confirmed every time we lie or cheat.

The coffin wasn't much—a Reebok shoebox—but for Fluffy it was more than adequate. I took a plastic shovel, dug a hole in the woods behind my house, and put my hamster in the ground. For weeks, his lifeless body lingered in my mind. I ate little and slept little. And I *was* little—little enough to discover that there was something fundamentally wrong with me. In class, my mind wandered back to my house, through the family room where I watched TV, to the yard where a trail leads to the entrance of the woods. I still go there today.

When I consider the question, why do bad things happen to good people? I think of Fluffy. I think of the crime I committed against God's creature. No one is good, not even a six-year-old boy (*especially* not a six-year-old boy). We humans are born with venom in our veins, injected by our great ancestors Adam and Eve and confirmed every time we lie or cheat. If we are born deserving punishment, we can't accuse God of being unjust by allowing bad things to happen to bad people. Like a comic-book villain who deserves defeat, we, too, fight against God. According to Paul, we were God's enemy when He captured us by grace (Romans 5:10). Now, if bad things happened to good people, we might raise our eyebrows and shake our fists at God. But the disease of depravity runs so thickly through our nature that our only cry must be, "Give me grace or else I die."

Since bad things do happen to people, God gives Christians grace to be His hands and hearts to those who face affliction. "'Comfort, oh comfort my people,' says your God" (Isaiah 40:1). When Jesus Christ was on earth, He preached the coming of the kingdom of God. Many believed it was a future event—a distant deliverance. The disciples believed this coming kingdom would be a political liberation, since Jerusalem was under Roman occupation. This is why Peter takes out his sword to defend Jesus before the arrest (Matthew 26:51). King Herod, too, felt his earthly kingdom threatened by the birth of a Messiah King and sought to assassinate Him.

the person and power of Christ penetrate the present.

Christians believe that one day God's kingdom will come "on earth as it is in heaven" (Matthew 6:10 NIV), but it also has already arrived. When Jesus walked our earth, He ushered the kingdom of God into the world through preaching the gospel, saving the lost, and healing the sick. The person and power of Christ penetrate the present. The glory of God is brought into our present circumstances, and through the Holy Spirit we're given power to accomplish God's will in this world. In other words, Christians don't have to wait for God to lock Satan in his dungeon; we can go ahead and claim the victory, preach the gospel, fight for social justice, and be the hands and heart of God for those who sink into despair. It is heaven in the here and now.

Since we are followers of Christ and operate in His name, we too usher the kingdom of God into this world. Every time we minister the gospel, feed the hungry, care for the sick, and comfort the dying, we are bringing the *what will be* into the *what is*. This is why demons feared the ministry of Jesus so much. They knew who they were dealing with.

Once Jesus got into the boat with His disciples (Luke 8:22). A storm arose on the lake, but Jesus was sleeping beneath the bow. The water was white with foam; the disciples were white with fear. Yet Jesus rebuked the wind and dropped an Alka-Seltzer in the waves. All was calm. And the disciples wondered, "Who is this man that even the wind and the waves obey Him?"

A little later Jesus encountered a demon-possessed man. He was a man who lived among the tombs, a satanic Superman—too strong to be chained, too powerful to be subdued. Yet Jesus rebuked the demons and sent them into a herd of kamikaze pigs. And the disciples wondered, "Who is this man that even the demons obey Him?"

No doubt the demons knew who Jesus was, which is why they were running away with their curly tails between their legs. They knew He was the God who held eternity in His hands, who calmed storms, walked on water, and judged creatures great and small. They knew this man was not just another prophet; He was the very Word of God. He was not just another priest; He was the Lamb to be slain. He was not just a king; He was the King of all kings.

So when we act like Christians, we become salt and light in a dark and bland world. But what is the best way to comfort those who suffer? Rarely with words. There are no easy answers to life's troubling problems, and the right answer at the wrong time is still the wrong answer. When Job was suffering, his friends sat with him for three days before saying a word. When they did open their mouths, their words brought more harm than help, but we can learn a lesson from them—the art of listening. People are dying for someone to listen. Not only must we listen; we must also make ourselves vulnerable enough to mourn with those who mourn (Romans 12:15). Sympathy without empathy is simply pity. Sure,

when people suffer, they need someone to cry with, be with, and hurt with.

there will be a day for answers, a day for theological interrogations. But in the moment of pain, when all is dark and dead in our lives, we usher in the kingdom of God by *being*, not by *saying*.

When people suffer, they may say that they're fine, but they want us to feel their pain. They want someone to suffer with them, someone who understands what they're going through. When people hurt, they don't need books on the abstract concept of suffering and how that theologically relates to the goodness of God. They don't need casual "hellos" and "how are yous?" They need someone to cry with, be with, and hurt with.

One of the greatest poets and hymn writers, William Cowper, experienced terrible depression throughout his life. Born into a family of poets in England, it's not surprising that he put so much of his misery on paper.

> Me miserable! how could I escape
> Infinite wrath and infinite despair!
> Whom Death, Earth, Heaven, and Hell consigned to ruin,
> Whose friend was God, but God swore not to aid me![2]

Cowper suffered from tremendous moodiness and on a few occasions he was even assigned to an asylum. Once he attempted suicide. A close friend and listening ear, John Newton, the hymn writer of "Amazing Grace," encouraged Cowper as best he knew how. In November 1792, Cowper wrote to Newton, "I seem to myself to be scrambling always in the dark, among rocks and precipices without a guide, but with an enemy ever at my heels, prepared to push me headlong."[3]

Years of depression reduced William Cowper to a man who had no confidence. Sad and shy, he sought a place to be alone. But one day, after a severe emotional battle, Cowper found a baby rabbit. It was injured to the extent that Cowper felt compelled to take care of it. The small children of Olney, his village, saw that he not only tended to the animal, but tamed it. Word spread throughout the town of his kindness, and soon he was practically running a zoo at his house. He had guinea pigs and squirrels, cats and dogs, ducks and hens, and many other creatures.

Cowper's ability to focus on something that needed more help than he did soothed his spirit and gave him a reason to live. Month after month his interest in animals escalated, and he began to notice how cruel humanity was toward these creatures. Biographer George Melvyn Ella noted, "Cowper was one of the first poets of the eighteenth century to argue for a display of human feeling to be shown to animals."[4] And in his poem "On a Goldfinch Starved to Death in His Cage," Cowper spoke out against cruelty to God's creatures.[5]

While Cowper certainly never murdered a hamster, he did understand the sin in his heart. He took it very seriously, knowing that it was within his power to commit terrible acts of hatred. He knew the consequences of being born in rebellion against God and wrote about it: "My God, how perfect are thy ways! But mine polluted are."[6] In his poem "God Shall Be All in All," he wrote, "By [Adam's] own fault he forfeits happiness both for himself and for his descendants."[7]

It was in the darkness that Cowper discovered the light of God. He wrote poems and sermons that exalted the redeeming work of Christ and the power of God to forever heal the heart. Through his writings, he communicated the doctrines of grace with great clarity and effectiveness:

Lord, I believe thou has prepar'd
(Unworthy tho' I be)
For me a blood-bought free reward,
A golden harp for me.[8]

The hymns Cowper composed are seasoned with spices of suffering and saturated with theology. Throughout the years they have encouraged people who have suffered in various ways. His words remind us that death is a reality of life . . . and they give hope to six-year-old hamster killers like myself who need God's grace every day. They even address the age-old question, why do bad things happen to good people? But most importantly, these sacred songs testify to the greatness of the God who does not let His children walk through dark places without going before them, behind them, and beside them.

By the end of his life, Cowper had learned to sing through the storms. His voice was loud and strong, confident that God inflicted injury on Christ so humanity would forever be cured. And in one of his most famous hymns, "God Moves in a Mysterious Way," Cowper bears witness to the discovery of worship in the midst of suffering and depression:

God moves in a mysterious way
His wonders to perform;
He plants His footsteps in the sea

And rides upon the storm.

You fearful saints, fresh courage take:
The clouds you so much dread
Are big with mercy, and shall break
In blessings on your head.

Judge not the Lord by feeble sense,
But trust Him for His grace;
Behind a frowning providence
He hides a smiling face.

His purposes will ripen fast,
Unfolding every hour;
The bud may have a bitter taste,
but sweet will be the flower.[9]

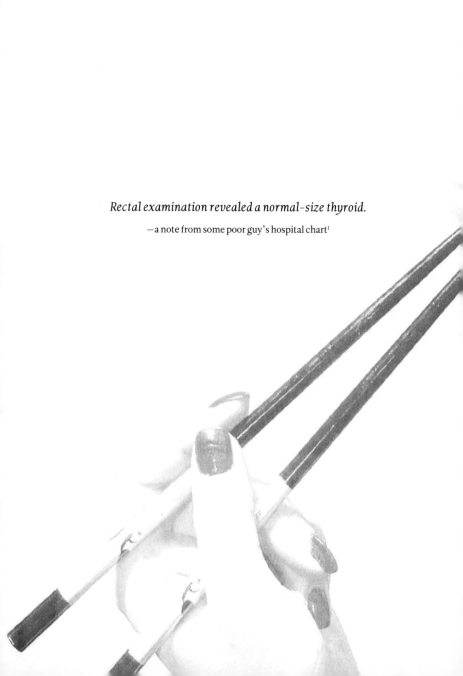

Rectal examination revealed a normal-size thyroid.

—a note from some poor guy's hospital chart[1]

grappling
with
God

BEING A GUY is a smelly thing—blood, sweat, and socks that reek of sludge. I remember flying through a dense Alabama forest on a four-wheeler—twenty, thirty, forty miles an hour—sliding on trails that were much too muddy. Fat raindrops sizzled on the hot Honda engine as bouts of sunshine interrupted the downpour. The trail was sloshed with mud, and we were caked in it too. Wearing only boxers, we sped through the trees, up hills, and over bridges that rattled beneath our weight.

It was Saturday, and even our souls were getting wet, wet from recycled water that had splashed so many high school students before. But we didn't care. Caring is for those who have something to do. But all we had to do was to pluck the pieces of pine straw from our lips and jump into the lake that was as muddy as Mississippi Pie.

Maybe it's the testosterone flowing through my veins, but there's something inside me that enjoys the sweat, blood, and tears of a good fight. Any competitive sport will do. Boxing, wrestling, football, martial arts—I'll take them all. As boys, we are wired to wrestle and geared to grapple. As we get older, our bodies are coated with armor in the form of muscle.

In the spirit of *Fight Club*, after a long day at school, there are few things I enjoy more than a good brawl with my buddies—no gloves, no-holds-barred, and certainly no sissy punches. Since both body and brain must be exercised, I've found that martial arts is a challenging discipline. Yeah, I'll get bruised, kicked, subdued, or even put to sleep with one of those "rear naked chokes," but there's nothing that draws guys together like three five-minute rounds in the ring.

WRESTLING WITH AN ANGEL

In the Old Testament, a man named Jacob wrestled an angel. Paralyzed at the thought of meeting his brother Esau, Jacob was unable to sleep. During the night he took his family and crossed the river Jabbok, and after making sure they were safe, Jacob found himself alone. As he walked through the desert, Jacob felt a hand grab his shoulder. It wasn't a normal hand but a fierce one. Spinning around, Jacob swung at the creature, who ducked and responded with an uppercut.

Back and forth they fought, exchanging blows and blood. Jacob threw a flying knee at the creature's rib cage, but it was blocked and reciprocated with an elbow to the jaw. Falling to the ground, Jacob kicked the legs out from under the creature. His opponent anticipated the action and flipped Jacob onto his back, slamming his head against the ground.

Jacob was a tough guy. But as he wrestled with this creature, he realized that he had bitten off more than he could chew. While he could put a normal man on his back in a matter of seconds, he sensed that he wasn't fighting a normal man. For hours they struggled, muscle to muscle, their sweat making slippery the skin they tried to bruise. Every strike was returned, every kick deflected. It was as if Jacob were wrestling with God Himself. And suddenly, as the morning light licked the sand-covered bodies, the creature dislocated Jacob's hip and stood to its feet as the winner.

Wrapping his arms around the creature's leg, Jacob wouldn't release his death grip until the creature blessed him. This was the first time Jacob had ever been beaten, yet he wanted the victor to reward his valiant effort.

"What is your name?" the creature asked.

"Jacob."

The creature looked down at him. He knew that the name Jacob meant "deceiver," and perhaps knew that in his youth Jacob had stolen his brother's birthright. "Your name will no longer be Jacob, but Israel, because you have struggled with God and with men and have overcome." Limping away, Jacob called the place "Penial" because he saw God's face and lived (Genesis 32:30; for the full story, read 32:6-31).

Aikido is a Japanese martial art system based on harmony and dynamic circular momentum. In my third year of studying it, I learned a hip throw called *aiki otoshi* that can be used against any attacker. After evading an initial strike, perhaps a punch or kick, you slide your hips parallel to the hips of your aggressor and maintain a low and stable stance. As you grab his legs, his weight will be channeled through your leg into the ground, splitting his balance in half. Then you remove his legs from the ground and throw them over your hips.

Aiki otoshi is a very effective neutralization technique that can be implemented on anyone, regardless of weight or size. In fact, this technique is so efficient that six- and seven-year-olds can perform it against adults and make them look like rag dolls in the hands of a puppet master.

Did God perform *aiki otoshi* against Jacob? Perhaps. The One who made the body certainly knows how to break it. The body itself is a fragile organism. It takes minimum effort to break a nose or crack a rib, and even the most well-trained boxer isn't strong enough to perform at his peak for more than several rounds. How did Jacob struggle against God's angel for the entirety of the night? Think about the bruises, cuts, and swollen lips. Imagine the groans uttered, the techniques utilized, and the hopes of Jacob dashed to pieces in the dirt. When the final bell rang, after the grueling dueling, God walked away as the victor of the fight. And for the first time in his life, Jacob limped home, defeated and sweaty yet blessed and transformed.

Having studied three forms of martial arts—jeet kune do, karate, and aikido, I've discovered that you never really know someone until you fight them. It's only in the heat of battle that true character emerges. It's only in the tough times, the dirty and bloody times, that true weaknesses surface and true friendships solidify. Battlefields have a way of uniting soldiers, and so do boot camps, classrooms, hospitals, and cemeteries. The harder the struggle, the more deeply we depend on those around us.

Jacob wasn't the only one who wrestled with God. We all do. We all struggle against the Savior. Paul said that before we were made alive in Christ we were dead in our sins (Ephesians 2:5). We were zombies, dead and decaying yet active and hostile. But Christ engaged us in strange combat. We swung at God, our hollow eyes fixed on Him. We screeched in His face, our breath reeking of dead things. We wrapped our arms around Him, throwing fists at His head. Our bloated bellies leaked with bile and sin as we tried to kill Him. And though God could have put bullets in our brains, He chose to remove the obstacles between us. Hour by hour He warmed our cold hearts, pinning our elbows to our side and swirling us around with beautiful force. We tried to scratch out His eyes, but He gently redirected the attack. We tried to bite His arm, but He lovingly restrained our aggression. Like a kung fu master, He wrapped us up.

HOW WE GRAPPLE WITH GOD

For years we struggled with Him, denying His existence, avoiding His churches, and hating His followers. But at last, when our own strength failed, we began to feel a tingle in our arms and a prickle in our legs. Our heart began pumping blood, our lungs began breathing air, and warmth spread throughout the organs of our guts. C. S. Lewis wrote, "Every story of conversion is the story of a blessed defeat,"[2] and God gives grace to His gruesome monsters.

Even after we are saved, we grapple with God. We arm ourselves with pride, selfishness, and disobedience. We purchase the metal of materialism and coat ourselves with it. We wear the chain mail of sexual sins and take up our shield of independence. Yet God is no stranger to combat, and His Holy Spirit convicts us with arrows shot into the weak places of our armor. The Christian is a torn creature.

While our bodies of sin rot and decay, God has awakened another force within us, a passion for purity. It is this quest that pumps us to know Him fully, serve Him faithfully, and love Him with every ounce of our existence.

As we engage His Word, we grapple with its truths. How do we reconcile the differences among the Gospels and the apparent contradictions throughout the Scriptures? How can Jesus be in heaven, yet He says He will be with us on earth? How many times did the rooster crow after Peter denied Jesus? How long was Jesus in the tomb? Did Judas really hang himself, or did his intestines explode at the bottom of a cliff?

A hundred and fifty years ago, the Western world prided itself on its scientific knowledge. Darwin's new theory hit the press, railways were being laid throughout the world, and electricity sparked great ideas in the minds of those like Thomas Edison. The Christian community basked in this newly enlightened age and sought to understand the Bible in those terms. While great energy was spent exploring the Old and New Testaments, some biblical scholars attempted to view God's Word through scientific lenses. They reduced the miracles and mysteries of the Scriptures to folklores and myths because they couldn't reproduce or understand them. Karl Barth (1886-1968), the greatest theologian of the twentieth century, was schooled in this system of thought and violently opposed it. At the end of his life, after years of faithful preaching and teaching, Barth was asked to summarize his theology in one sentence. After thinking for a moment, he said, "Jesus loves me; this I know, for the Bible tells me so."

we do grapple with the mysteries of the Bible. did a great fish really eat jonah?

There are still remnants of the historical-critical movement in our universities and college campuses. Professors trained in disemboweling the Bible divorce personal devotion to Christ from academic biblical scholarship and plant seeds of doubt in the minds and hearts of those seeking the meaning of Scripture. Modern scholarship, however, is showing that such thinking is exhausted, dehydrated, and outdated.

Nevertheless, we do grapple with the mysteries of the Bible. Did a great fish really eat Jonah? How could Jonah have survived three days surrounded by sin and seaweed? When I was a kid I really couldn't figure this out. I thought it was just a fairy tale like Santa Claus or the Easter Bunny. But I remember a preacher saying to me, "Christian, do you believe God could make a whale?"

I nodded.

"And do you think God could make a man?"

Again I nodded.

"Then why can't God put them together?"

For years I've pondered his words. If I really believe that God can work His providential power and create matter from nothing, I should have no problem when He wants to bend His rules. God is not limited even by His own ordinances, and when I question God's ability to perform miracles, my own salvation comes into question, for that is the greatest miracle of all.

I often struggled to reconcile the differences among the four Gospels. I studied every text that seemed contradictory and read endless commentaries. But I remember walking through the van Gogh museum in Amsterdam, looking at his paintings. He, too, was the son of a preacher who enjoyed art. In fact, he was an expert at impressionism—a style of art that portrays reality through the expression of light. He mixed colors in fascinating ways and reproduced landscapes with great skill. As I walked by his colorful work, I passed fields of wheat crunched beneath clouds of pink and purple. I saw tree trunks twisting from their roots to branches that forked through the swirling sky. And I remember, in particular, a series of paintings. The subject remained the same, but each scene was painted during a different time of day. So the same rock, for instance, looked one way in the morning and another in the evening. The scenery didn't change, but the shadows, colors, and hues did.

All four Gospel writers painted the life of Jesus Christ in different lights. In their own unique ways they emphasized different aspects of His life because they were writing to different audiences. Matthew paints Christ in the morning. He begins with a long genealogy and birth story. Mark paints Christ in the afternoon. He takes no time to sketch the early years but hits the ground running at the hot height of Christ's ministry. Luke paints Christ in the evening. It is the longest gospel, coupled with Acts, meticulously portraying the Last Supper and the evening in the garden of Gethsemane. John paints Christ in the midnight. When all the world was dark with sin and doubt, Jesus Christ pierced the blackness and showed Himself as the light and hope of humanity. On its own, each gospel appears isolated and disconnected, but when viewed together, as the Holy Spirit delivered them to us, they represent a multidimensional picture of the life of Jesus, a three-dimensional portrait of His nature. And such a work of art demands our response of admiration and worship.

NAKED WRESTLING

For Greeks, there were three categories of combat sports: boxing, wrestling, and pankration (a mixture of the two). In 776 B.C. the Olympic Games began in Greece, and combat sports like these were demonstrated for prizes. In the late sixth century, Milo of Croton became the greatest athlete to champion these forms, winning the Olympic Games six times in a row. Among the ancient civilizations that practiced combat sports, the Greeks were unique because they competed in the nude.

Fighting naked had several benefits. The enemy couldn't take your clothes as trophies to their cities if they killed you, as was customary, and it's easier to fight without cumbersome clothes weighing you down. The Vikings discovered this strategy many centuries later and would often rub oil on their naked bodies before going out to battle. The author of Hebrews pleaded, "Strip down, start running — and never quit" (Hebrews 12:1).

Paul also understood this. When he lived in Corinth for a year and a half, he would have seen the Isthmian games. Like the Olympic, Nemean, and Pythian games, the Isthmian games celebrated the beauty of the body, the talent of the competitors, and the skills of the winner. Many presume that Paul was making tents for this very purpose when he lived there, since many people would need shelter on the outskirts of Corinth. In his letter to the Christians in Corinth, Paul wrote:

> Do you not know that in a race all the runners run, but only one gets the prize? Run in such a way as to get the prize. Everyone who competes in the games goes into strict training. They do it to get a crown that will not last, but we do it to get a crown that will last forever. Therefore I do not run like a man running aimlessly; I do not fight like a man beating the air. No, I beat my body and make it my slave so that after I have preached to others, I myself will not be disqualified for the prize. (1 Corinthians 9:24–27 NIV)

I often question my dedication as a follower of God. Do I train like a fighter for my faith, or am I a couch-potato Christian? Do I want to receive the prize, or am I fine with mediocrity? Have I made my body a slave to Christ, or am I still chained to the flesh?

Sometimes I act like being a Christian is like having a bank account where I withdraw funds when I need them. Or perhaps it's like owning a bar of soap that cleans my dirtiest parts. But the secret to Christianity is not about the materialistic trappings; it's about living in the presence of God. It's not about my opinion of God; it's about God's opinion of me. Am I carving out time in my day for prayer, Bible study, and meditation? Am I willing to lay it all on the line for my faith?

Only by cultivating a constant awareness of God's company in our lives do we find spiritual satisfaction. When we're taking a shower, we praise God for sprinkling us with grace. When we're eating breakfast, we worship the giver of good things. When we're driving down the road, we thank Him for signs that lead to godliness. Paul once wrote, "Don't shuffle along, eyes to the ground, absorbed with the things right in front of you. Look up, and be alert to what is going on around Christ—that's where the action is. See things from his perspective" (Colossians 3:2). And by daily doing so, we are training for the race we're called to run.

Christ isn't a sleepy spectator, watching us run from His throne in heaven. He's not in the bleachers, cheering us on from beyond the clouds. Rather, Jesus is wearing His jersey and He's running beside us, strengthening our spirits and encouraging us to keep going. Even though we often feel that we are the first to run the race, Christ has laid down the footprints we are called to follow, and we can run as though we can win.

As the Romans gained prominence in the world, they found the Greek form of fighting abhorrent. It was beneath them to wrestle in the nude, and instead they fought in loincloths. As a way of commemorating the triumph of their civilization over the chaotic nature of wild beasts, they built Roman amphitheaters in which gladiatorial combat occurred. Almost every Roman city had an amphitheater for these bloody bouts between soldiers. Animals, too, were forced to fight in these arenas—elephants, lions, deer, bears, crocodiles, seals, bulls, rhinoceroses, and more.[3]

During the first century, Nero set fire to Rome and blamed the Christians for it. Massive persecution occurred, and Christians were martyred before huge crowds. The historian Josephus records that many Christians were placed inside the skins of animals so that wild dogs would tear them apart.[4] Emperor Nero burned Christians alive and used them as lamps for his gardens. Both Peter and Paul apparently were put to death under the authority of Nero, whose bloodlust was as advanced as his insanity.

Not long ago I found myself walking through the Roman Colosseum, where many Christians had given their lives for the gospel. I tried to imagine how it must have been—the white marble, the screaming crowds, and the sound of animal jaws chomping at their victims. Jesus once told His disciples, "If they beat on me, they will certainly beat on you" (John 15:20), and as big as the Colosseum was, my respect for the Christians who died there was bigger.

> deep down, I knew that there was nothing Christian about the american dream, even though it still shines brightly in my eyes.

For many years, the American dream captured my attention. It goes something like this: paying off a house, owning two or three nice cars, investing in the stock market, joining a country club, and eventually dying a peaceful death. I encountered this ideology in pulpits, podcasts, books, and magazines. It's a comfortable Christianity, a faith of luxury and security. I remember even getting on my knees once or twice, praying for it.

Yet there was no room for a dream like this within the circular walls of the Colosseum. Where does martyrdom fit into this dream? What about suffering or evangelism? Deep down, I knew that there was nothing Christian about the American dream, even though it still shines brightly in my eyes. While there's nothing inherently evil about being rich and living a comfortable life, Christ urges us to take seriously a life of ultimate surrender.

True Christianity is a call to die. It's a call to die to our sinful passions and detach ourselves from pride. It's a call to be suspicious of comfort zones that rust our spiritual armor. But it's also a call to live, not in the center of ourselves but on the edge of things, on the fringe of things. To live with those who have little to lose and little to love, to "know Christ personally, experience his resurrection power, be a partner in his suffering, and go all the way with him to death itself" (Philippians 3:10).

That's the life I envisioned as I exited the Colosseum. That's the life the early Christians lived, and I thought of all the women and children who loved Christ more than earthly freedom. I thought of the young men who valued Jesus of Nazareth more than a few more decades on this globe. And every time I see a picture of the Colosseum, I hear them say, "Step up, Christian, and be a man of God for a change."

CHRISTIAN SAMURAI

On August 15, 1549, a Jesuit named Francis Xavier landed on the shores of Japan. He was well received by the local Japanese and converted them to Christianity in great numbers. In his diary he wrote, "It seems to me that we shall never find among heathens another race to equal the Japanese."[5] Indeed, the Japanese were an impressive people. Torn between shame and honor, they strove for excellence in all that they did. While Christian missionary efforts never really penetrated Japan as a whole, Xavier found great success among the samurai.

In Japanese, *samurai* means "to serve," and these were warriors who served the aristocracy. Eventually they took the government from the aristocracy and called themselves *bushi*, which means "warrior."[6] They developed fighting styles and took their training very seriously, though they were also skilled in music, art, and poetry. From 1467 to 1567, political instability characterized the Japanese landscape as warlords fought for territory and power. It was during this Era of the Warring States that Francis Xavier converted many samurai armies. The samurai were attracted to Christians because of the commonality of discipline and obedience. The detachment of worldly things, the ability to focus one's mind on something greater, and the quest for ultimate truth drew the samurai to the saints, and there are even stories of samurai armies carrying crosses into battle.

Christianity permeated every aspect of the samurai's life, including the battlefield. And so, in 1567, Shibata Katsuie led his samurai army against Miyoshi and Matsunaga. The battle occurred near the city of Sakai, in midwest Japan, where Father Luis Fróis was sharing the gospel of Jesus Christ. It was Christmas Eve, and as the two armies gathered at Sakai, Father Fróis invited them to take the Lord's Supper. The samurai armies came together and shared the supper, calling one another brothers in Christ—before returning to their camps in preparation of the battle.[7]

One of the guiding principles of the Code of Bushido, the samurai code of ethics and warfare, is to "keep death in mind at all times, every day and every night, from the morning of New Year's Day through the night of New Year's Eve."[8] Christians have much to learn about discipline and mind-set, even from secular books like this. What would happen if we developed a keen awareness of our own mortality? Would we love God with greater fervency? Would we support missionaries with greater generosity? Would we govern our thoughts, words, and actions with greater care? I think about the Christians who took the gospel to Japan. Many were martyred by the very samurai they tried to convert, but in their death they showed the Japanese people how a Christian dies, and thousands were converted in the shade of their crosses.

Christians are bullets in God's barrel. The bullet has no right to say to the barrel, "Hey, point me in that direction," or "Aim me over there." Our responsibility is simple—to say, "Wherever He shoots, I'll go."

I once dated a girl whose grandfather discouraged our relationship because I told him that God might be calling me to the mission field in Africa. "You could get yourself killed over there, son," he said. "Or worse—you could get my granddaughter killed! Don't take that kind of chance!"

> words like *chance, accident,* and *happenstance* don't belong in a Christian's vocabulary.

That relationship didn't last long, and I became convinced that words like *chance, accident,* and *happenstance* don't belong in a Christian's vocabulary. In fact, I even cut them out of my dictionary. Right now the church in America needs parents who are willing to release their children to the mission field. We need parents who love God more than their children. In ancient times, when two armies met each other on the battlefield, it was assumed that those who were fighting on the front lines would be killed the quickest. Yet, parents sent their teenagers to the front line because they understood the seriousness of winning the war. Are we willing to do the same? Are we able to say with the Spartans, "Come back with your shield or on it"? If we recognize the importance of evangelism, we will encourage future generations to give their lives for God and enter the heat of the battlefield even in the face of great danger.

Nothing happens outside of God's arrangements. Being a soccer player, I remember watching a video of Pelé, the greatest player in the history of the game, juggle a grapefruit on his foot for several minutes. It astonished me how he could control the piece of fruit. With obedience the grapefruit followed the direction of its master. In fact, everything that was round found familiarity with Pelé's foot, and he magically shamed his opponents as he dribbled the soccer ball down the field. God controls our earth even more than Pelé controlled a soccer ball. God spins our planet according to His design. He kicks it, stops it, and bends it like Beckham[9] around the universe. God said, "Heaven is my throne room; I rest my feet on earth" (Acts 7:49), and if He controls the earth, he certainly controls our destinies.

When I was a kid my sister dared me to ride my bike down the driveway without holding on to the handlebars. It was actually a triple-dog-dare, so I had to do it. Halfway down the steep concrete, I lost control of the bike and fell headfirst over the handlebars onto the pavement. During the three weeks that it took for the scabby strawberries to heal on my hands and knees, I decided that I wanted to skate through life without getting hurt. The smoother the ride, the better. For those few weeks I would make my goal to feel only as much pain as absolutely necessary. To that end, I didn't take chances. I flinched at bungee jumping, hang gliding, and Indian food. I avoided, as best I could, holding my breath too long under water. I wanted to slide into heaven without even a bruise on my knee.

This is a common teaching in our culture. But Christians aren't called to self-preservation; rather, we're called to combat the forces of darkness, the powers of our flesh, and the temptations of the world. Like soccer players, our job is simply to move the ball downfield. We aren't called to hoard the ball or bury it beneath the turf. We must move it in the right direction. This was Francis Xavier's calling, Martin Luther's calling, Charles Spurgeon's calling, and our calling too. We must fight the temptation to savor the spotlight and learn to accept the bruises and shoves that come from our opponents' attack. With great skill we must pass the faith of our fathers to future generations who are waiting for us down the field.

I still enjoy riding four-wheelers, though I usually wear more than just boxers these days. Sometimes when I'm stuck in class listening to a lecture, I'll close my eyes and feel the wind against my face. I'll remember the sharp rain against my eyes and the thrill of doing doughnuts in circles of mud. I don't take death seriously anymore. Why should I? Death is nothing more than a stingray without a stinger, a toothless shark gumming us into the presence of Christ.

For now, I continue grappling with God, but I know that no matter how slippery sin makes me, His grip on me is good, and a day is coming when brawling will turn to bawling and I will embrace the One who embraced the cross on my behalf.

If you guys ever have kids and one of them when he's eight years old accidentally sets fire to the living room rug . . . go easy on him.

—**MARTY MCFLY** in *Back to the Future*

back
to the
future

THE HUMAN BODY was made to move forward. Anatomically, our eyes are located in the front of our faces, our arms and elbows bend forward, and even our knee and ankle joints propel us ahead. Intellectually, we are encouraged to think and plan for the future—future finances, future investments, and future career strategies, for example. And bookshelves are bloated with books about how to find a future mate in six months or less. Religiously, we're also taught to focus on the future. No matter what we've done in the past, or how bad we've been to our friends, the future is what matters to God.

Physically, intellectually, and spiritually we are a forward-looking people.

But if our faith is to be healthy, we must look to the past before we look to the future. We must take a step back in order to take a step forward. We must go back to the Bible and the roots of our faith. We must rediscover the ancient doctrines, creeds, and confessions that enrich our Christian heritage. We must listen to the hymns that history has sung for us long ago; sit under the teachings of the Council of Nicea, the Apostles' Creed, and the Westminster Confession; read the writings of St. Augustine and John Wesley; understand Julian of Norwich and Jonathan Edwards; and learn the sermons of John Bunyan and D. L. Moody. Though these people have long since died, they still speak to us, instructing our faith and encouraging our lives. Only when we review the past can we preview the future.

why settle for Hershey's Kisses when the chocolate factory is ours for the eating?

When I was a kid I thought heaven was a cloudy candy land, a blurry place of sugar bliss where angels ate jellybeans by streets of Easter bunnies and M&Ms. Christians, too, were in my heaven, filling their stomachs with Popsicles before jumping on trampolines that stretched the stars. It was a magical place, a future place, a place of sunsets and Slip 'n Slides.

But heaven will be better than that. Instead of having an inner itching for sinful behavior, we'll yearn and burn for Christ. God will suck the poison from His people, and we'll be consumed with a passion for worship. We will applaud God for redeeming us, pulsing and praising His name. Heaven won't be a giant golf course where saints follow a ball from one cloud to another. Nor will it be an amusement park where roller coasters dip and soar through sky and space. Heaven will be a place where Christians adore the Christ who sacrificed Himself to satisfy the deepest longings of our hearts.

For now, we are pilgrims in a land that is not our home. We press on toward our final destination as strangers on this earth. Instead of living for the weekend or partying your life away, give yourself to something great. Abandon the American dream of health and wealth and risk your life for the kingdom of God. Let's pray a little harder and love a little more. There are already too many wasted lives in this world. Nothing is more gratifying than soaking up the Savior and splashing others with His glory. Nothing is so rewarding as sleeping with a clean and forgiven conscience. C. S. Lewis wrote, "We are halfhearted creatures, fooling about with drink and sex and ambition when infinite joy is offered us."[1] Why settle for less than perfect communion with Christ? Why settle for Hershey's Kisses when the chocolate factory is ours for the eating?

The face of Christianity is currently undergoing plastic surgery, a face-lift, in fact. The flesh of our faith is changing—the style of worship, the technology used, and the songs that are sung. But we must never abandon the bone structure behind the skin—our belief in the unified three-person God, our embrace of grace alone by faith alone in Christ alone, and our commitment to the supremacy of Holy Scripture. These are nonnegotiable for Christians. Everything else may change—the eyebrows, freckles, wrinkles, and dimples—but the contours of our Christianity must not. The theology of the past must be minted to coins of the present. And by doing so, spiritual revival will sweep our society.

These days, there is an emerging interest in Jesus, but there is also a reaction against His church. People are crazy for Christ but want nothing to do with organized church. While this is a popular and widespread trend, we must be careful to keep the head of Christ attached to the body of Christ, lest we live a decapitated Christianity. God fulfilled our desires for community by encouraging us to come together as a church and worship, foreshadowing the great gathering of God's people in heaven.

Knowing God is like peeling an onion. Day by day we unfold His blessings. We encounter layers of love we never knew existed, levels of mercy that blow our minds away. Peel after peel, we uncover His attributes. There is graciousness, kindness, power, and jealousy. We discover His glory and splendor. We agree with the psalmist that God "poured great draughts of water down parched throats; the starved and hungry got plenty to eat" (Psalm 107:9). After tasting the Lord's kindness, we get closer to the center of the Savior and find His heart full of sacrifice. And the whole peeling process, the whole salvation story, has made our eyes water with tears of humility and repentance.

LEANING AGAINST THE WIND

Iona, an island off the coast of Scotland, is a mystical land that thousands of pilgrims have visited. The Celts called it a "thin place" because the boundary between earth and heaven is blurred on its shores. For being so thin, I found it thick with spiritual blessing.

One day I decided to walk across the island. Having no map or guide, I quickly became lost and found myself wandering through the northeastern hills. The wind on the island of Iona can be fierce. At times, gale-force winds blow in from the sea at forty and even fifty miles an hour. I certainly faced them as I climbed up the grassy hills. Most of the time I found shelter from the violent gusts, but every now and again, they slammed into me and nearly knocked me off my feet.

I remember climbing up one hill in particular; from its slopes I could see the water of Port Ban. When I arrived at the top, I stood to my feet and admired the view. The wind was forceful in my face, winsome and wild. Looking to see if anyone was watching, I removed my backpack and let it fall roughly against the ground. I could barely open my eyes from all the wind and sand thrashing against my skin, so I turned away from the water and spread wide my arms. To my amazement, I discovered that I could lean against the wind. Locking my limbs, I leaned hard against it and felt it leaning hard against me. It was invisible yet strangely powerful, a sustaining gust that pushed against my trunk.

I allowed gravity to encourage a fall, but the hardy wind held me there, resolved to keep me up. The violent breeze sustained my posture for about fifteen seconds before I curled to my knees and scrambled down the hill.

The rest of my hike became a nightmare. After asking directions, I kept the sea to my right but lost the trail and fell into a mud pit on the north side of the island. I almost drowned there in the sticky slough, as many pilgrims and cattle had previously done. It was the closest I've ever been to death, but God spared my life and I arrived at Saint Columba's Bay, where small green pebbles, unique to the island, lie.

Still, throughout the remainder of the day I felt the power of that gale-force wind blowing against my back. I felt the freedom of surrendering to something I couldn't see. And to this day I still feel its thrust against me.

My granddaddy once built an airplane. His family and friends said it couldn't be done. They said it was impossible to build a plane from scratch. But thirteen years later he sat in his cockpit, eyes on the skies and fist on the throttle, waiting for the rush of adrenaline that comes from breaking the threshold of gravity. In years to come he would win many aerial acrobatic competitions in his bright red Starduster biplane. But he didn't do it for the trophies or the glory or the satisfaction that comes from proving people wrong. He built his airplane because he loved the wind. He loved the way rudders work with side currents, the way propellers slice through skies like blades through butter. He loved doing loop-the-loops and barrel rolls, nosedives and chandelles. It was closer to heaven than most people get, and I think he saw God's glory better up there.

My grandmother earned her pilot's license too. She often worried that her husband would have a heart attack in the air, so she learned to fly his plane in case she needed to land it without him.

"But Grandma," I once said years later, "everybody has a time to die."

She looked at me and grinned. "Yes, but what if it was Granddaddy's time to die and not mine?"

She had a point. And my granddaddy did almost die as his biplane hovered above a Georgia cornfield. His engine had died at ten thousand feet and he lowered his altitude to gain airspeed, but it wasn't enough—six hundred feet, five hundred, four hundred. The ground was rising. All he could do was watch the altimeter swirl from life to death. As bits of corn sprayed across his cockpit window, his plane grazed the ground and bounced again into the air. The landing gear tore off and disappeared in the distance. My granddaddy's life flashed before his eyes—the savage fighting in the South Pacific, bullets piercing bodies, the smell of oil against melting flesh. It hadn't been an easy life, but he wasn't ready for it to end.

Finally the airplane slammed hard against the earth and flipped onto its top. The engine caught fire, the propellers blew off, and for Grandpa everything went black.

When the dust settled around the plane, he had broken some bones and lost some teeth but walked away with time still on the clock. His crash permanently scarred him, for good and for bad. Every morning when he put in those false teeth, he was reminded of God's mercy. Every evening he knew that God still had a purpose for him on this earth, and his scars testified to God's faithfulness. When we fished together on the Tennessee River, he always assured me that no matter how terrible my circumstances, nothing can prematurely take me from this world until God has accomplished His task with me here. My granddaddy's crash was one of the best blessings in his life, and he looked back to that experience to find meaning and purpose.

The past has a way of supporting the present. Though invisible, the ancient ways push against us, reminding us of all the Christians whom God upheld against the pressures of their day. The arms of God are strong, supporting us in times of turbulence. And no matter how disoriented we become, Christians lean against the Holy Spirit, the invisible One about whom Jesus said, "The wind blows wherever it pleases. You hear its sound, but you cannot tell where it comes from or where it is going" (John 3:8 NIV). And by leaning, we learn the way of love.

God leans against us too. Not for survival or support but for delight and pleasure. God created humanity to enjoy her. He gave us the desire for *intimacy* so He can love us, *community* so He can commune with us, and *eternity* so He can forever have and hold us. The Gardener leans against His trees and finds satisfaction in the breezes of their worship. Indeed, He planted us by streams of water (Psalm 1:3) so we could grow for Him. He nurtures us with sunshine so we can bear fruit for His lips. The Holy Spirit blows from tree to tree, from believer to believer, until the whole forest of God's creatures is fanning the One who reigns from the tree.

WHAT CATHEDRALS TELL US

One of the greatest things about traveling is walking into ancient cathedrals. Some are small, others tall. Some are frescoed, others plain. Some are golden, others bland. But all the cathedrals I've ever visited have one thing in common. They point to the past. They point beyond themselves. Even the gaudy ones make us consider immortality, heaven, and hell. The stained glass windows say, "Don't look at us; look through us and see God in all His shining splendor."

In Rome not so long ago, I entered the Basilica of Saint Paul Outside the Walls, a sanctuary that supposedly holds the bones of the apostle Paul. It was constructed in A.D. 384 over two marble slabs bearing the inscription *Paulo Apostolo Martyri* (Paul Apostle Martyr). Inside the sanctuary, my gaze was immediately raised to the ceiling, a flat Roman roof decorated in gold and art. Rows of columns line the nave of the cathedral, which climbs to the windows that usher sunlight onto the apse above the altar.

It was breathtaking. Poor pilgrim peasants must have fallen on their faces upon entering this church, thinking that heaven was represented in its walls.

As I walked through the massive building, not only were my head and neck turned upward, but also my thoughts. I looked at the art and considered the God who stretches sunsets across the canvas of His creation. I saw pictures of Jesus and His disciples and remembered His life, death, and resurrection. But most importantly I recognized that the world does not revolve around me. I was a small thing, standing there, small enough to be forgotten.

The cathedral reminded me that there was a greater narrative than my own short sentence. And I walked out of that sanctuary a little closer to the earth.

Christians need to know where we've been in order to know where we're going. We need to know about martyrs like Stephen, Peter, and Paul. We need to know about Perpetua, John Huss, and William Tyndale, for they, too, point us forward. They point beyond themselves, as John the Baptist did, to the Christ who laid down His life for His people and whose Crocs we are unworthy to unstrap. We have much to learn from those who were completely sold out to God, and whose testimonies encourage us to live as though we will live again.

THE CHURCH ON THE MOON

When I was a kid, one of my strangest dreams was to plant a church on the moon. I was going to call it First Baptist Moon and we would worship God with stars above and dust below. Of course there would be room for the Presbyterian, Methodist, and Anglican churches, but ours would be the wettest, with baptismal water floating and splashing the entire congregation. Sermons would be short enough to conserve the oxygen, and instead of Southern cooking buffet lines, we would eat fried chicken and cornbread from zip-locked bags of dehydrated astronaut food. And we would sing "All Creatures of Our God and King" with great zeal:

All creatures of our God and King,
Lift up your voice and with us sing,
Alleluia! Alleluia!
Thou burning sun with golden beam,
Thou silver moon with softer gleam!
O praise Him, O praise Him!
Alleluia, Alleluia, Alleluia![2]

Every day, the blue planet would cross our velvet sky and remind us of the past, when the love of God bled the Son of God for the people of God.

A DECISION TO MAKE

While the thought of being moon missionaries is exciting, the future of Christianity in America is growing uncertain. In his book *The Next*

Christendom, Philip Jenkins observed that global Christianity is shifting to the Southern Hemisphere.[3] South America and Africa are exploding with revival, while North America and Europe are declining in authentic faith. Having traveled throughout Europe, I can testify to this phenomenon. It seems to me like the church in America has a very important decision to make:

Either we revive or we rot.

Either we get on our knees and pray that God will spark another awakening in our land, or we become irrelevant to global Christianity.

> Jesus teaches us to grab life by the chopsticks and enjoy a fresher faith.

The past reminds us that the Christians of cultures who obtained great prosperity became too comfortable and their faith disintegrated as their Christianity spread to areas of persecution and need. It has been a long time since the faith of our fathers was tested, and we, the new and naive generation, know very little of the sacrifice that comes from giving our lives to God.

Nevertheless, we are learning. The past is teaching us how to behave. We are going back in order to go forward, and we're learning that it is costly to be a Christian. We are learning that true freedom comes from sacrifice, and obedience is more important than success. The way up is the way down, and darkness shows us Christ more than sunshine does. Instead of asking, "What would Jesus do?" we are asking, "What would Jesus have me do?"[4] And we are doing it. We are learning that God doesn't make mistakes. He doesn't call us to forget us. He doesn't equip us to discard us. And the God who pulls us to Himself joins us for the journey.

You don't have to be a writer to tell the story of Jesus. If you're an artist, paint it. If you're a singer, sing it. It doesn't matter what you do or where you are, every one of us can point beyond ourselves. If you are in retail, tell us about the transaction of salvation. If you are a gardener, describe His crown of thorns. If you are a mathematician, describe the length of the nails. Doctors can best portray His pain, and lawyers can best understand our pardon.

Jesus Christ is the hinge that holds us to heaven. He teaches us to grab life by the chopsticks and enjoy a fresher faith. He asks us to lean against His presence and trust what seems invisible. He is the past that ordains the future. He is the *beyond* in the midst of our *now*. And though we get a glimpse of God today, tomorrow we'll gaze at Him forever. For Christ has opened paradise and ushers us into eternity.

leap of faith

NO TURNING BACK. Time was ticking, and the smell of jet fuel filled my lungs. I boarded the twenty-seat, dual-engine aircraft. It was October and cold. As the plane taxied to the edge of the runway, I reassured myself that everything was going to be okay. *There's nothing to fear but fear itself.*

But what if my parachute doesn't open?

It was my father-in-law's fiftieth birthday, and he wanted to go skydiving, as George H. W. Bush had. I agreed to go with him but wanted out as the rush of speed hit my body. I wanted to be on the ground again where humans were created to live. But there I was, ears popping, stomach churning, about to jump out of a perfectly good airplane.

I peered through the foggy window as we rose above the clouds. Turbulence shook the airplane, sending streaks of panic down my spine. I hated turbulence. It was going to be a tandem jump; an instructor would be strapped to my back in case something went terribly wrong. And I could think of a million things that could go wrong!

"Remember," he told me, "keep your arms crossed over your shoulders. When we exit the plane, we'll fall for approximately four seconds. Then spread your arms out like I showed you."

I nodded.

"After that, we'll fall for seventy-five seconds. If you lean to your side, we'll spin around in circles. It you lean to your front, we'll accelerate. Be sure not to do that; we'll be going fast enough as it is." He suspected that I was nervous and forgetful, but he didn't know the half of it.

Our plane was filled with skydivers. Some wore leather, others spandex. One of the skydivers was drinking an energy drink, and before he jumped he cussed himself into a frenzy. Others joined in until the entire plane throbbed with profanity. Looking at the screaming skydivers, I wished that God would confuse their tongues for a moment, as He had those tower-climbers at Babel.

One by one the skydivers jumped, disappearing into the invisible deep and taking their words with them. It grew quieter in the plane until there was only one other guy remaining. He turned around and smirked at me, flicking his tongue as he fell backwards out the door. He was missing some teeth—couldn't imagine how that happened.

Finally it was my turn. I stood at the door of the plane, feeling the cold air against my face. "Put your goggles on," the instructor said. My shaky hands obeyed, and I almost wet myself but stopped for fear that a vertical trail of urine would follow me through the sky. The horizon curved in the distance, frowning at me for making this terrible decision. The ground was worlds away and looked like microscopic trees plastered to green construction paper. My breathing shallowed and my eyes widened, but I had passed the point of no return.

As I leaned into the wind, a calmness settled over me. It was a moment of perfect peace, a sunny morning moment that warms the soul before reality chills the flesh. It was a day when turbulence lost its terror and my fear met my faith.

I often go to that moment when all seems wrong and wicked in the world; when dreams run dry and passions shrink; when life tastes like meatloaf molding in the fridge. And suddenly I'm on the edge again, looking out at sky and space, waiting for God to wrap me in His arms. And the fall . . . well, that's another story altogether.

acknowledgments

Rebecca, who blushed at my title but thinks all three are great. Love you like crazy.

My parents, who showed me the pilgrim way.

Moody Publishers, especially Dave and Jim, among many others.

Brandon and Steve, who gave me Yoo-hoos before I beat them up.

The Mathis family, for letting me play in the cave.

Jason Donn, *moo-fah-sa.*

Sensei Bushnell, for the bow staff skills.

Anton, Elizabeth, and Alex Fourie, for your faithfulness.

Coach Chekwa, who taught me to play the game.

Brian Cosby and E.J. Waldron, scholars and friends.

Bill, Mac Guy *par excellence*, for troubleshooting my laptop.

Eric, the taxi driver in Indianapolis who got me there on time.

Snowball, my toothless Maltese. And Valentino, the Taco Bell rat dog from space.

Surin West in Birmingham, for the sushi.

Samford University's Mrs. Velma, for the chicken legs.

And Atlanta Skydiving Center, for the great landing.

Soli Deo Gloria

notes

Chapter 1–Russian Sex and Wedding Vows

1. "The Ode to the Sustaining of Friendship in a Relationship" was actually a statement of commitment that we both signed. It read: "This document serves as an agreement between two friends who dared to venture down the road of sustaining godliness in their friendship. By signing this agreement both individuals confirm their passion for purity and are responsible to God and one another to abide by the following commitments: To grow closer to God by maintaining a physically virtuous relationship. To pray with and for one another in all matters related to sexual desire. And to edify one another in Christ with love, respect, and mutual selflessness. May the God who brought you together hereby bless and ordain your friendship both now and forevermore. And now these three remain: faith, hope, and love. But the greatest of these is love. 1 Corinthians 13:13."
2. Robert Robinson, "Come Thou Fount of Every Blessing," in *Baptist Hymnal* (Nashville: Convention Press, 1991); in public domain.
3. Ibid., verse 3, line 2.
4. Teresa of Ávila, quoted in *Mystics, Visionaries, and Prophets: A Historical Anthology of Women's Spiritual Writings*, Shawn Madigan, ed. (Minneapolis: Fortress, 1988), 264.

Chapter 2–Naked with God

1. Michael de la Bedoyere, *Francis of Assisi: The Man Who Found Perfect Joy* (Manchester, N.H.: Sophia Institute Press, 1962), 68.
2. Ibid., 69.
3. *The Prayers of Saint Francis*, W. Bader, comp. (New York: New City Press, 1988), 21.
4. In 2007 Kobayashi ate a whopping sixty-three frankfurters despite a jaw injury; he lost to Joey Chestnut, who consumed sixty-six hot dogs.
5. *Francis and Clare: The Complete Works*, Regis J. Armstrong and Ignatius C. Brady, trans. (New York: Paulist Press, 1982), 103.

Chapter 3–Who's Your Daddy?

1. Baal-Zebub, mentioned in 2 Kings 1:2, means "Lord of the Flies."
2. Baal was "identified with the storm god Hadad, whose voice could be heard

in the reverberating thunder that accompanied rain," according to Merrill F. Unger, *The New Unger's Bible Dictionary*, R. K. Harrison, ed. (Chicago: Moody, 1988), 485.

3. John Pollock, *The Apostle: A Life of Paul* (New York: Doubleday, 1969), 115.

4. Martin Luther, "A Mighty Fortress Is Our God," in *Baptist Hymnal* (Nashville: Convention Press, 1991), 8.

5. Pliny the Elder, *Natural History*, Book 10, chaps. 3-6.

Chapter 4 - Selling Your Soul on eBay

1. Regarding its position in the body, Augustine wrote, "The soul is present as a whole not only in the entire mass of a body, but also in every least part of the body at the same time." See John W. Cooper, *Body, Soul, and Life Everlasting* (Grand Rapids: Eerdmans, 1989), 11. More recently, the Jivaro tribe in South America believed that the soul was found in the head, which is why they practiced the gruesome art of head shrinking.

2. *The Heidelberg Catechism: A New Translation* (Grand Rapids: Christian Reformed Board of Publications, 1975).

3. *Merriam-Webster's Collegiate Dictionary*, 11th ed., s.v. "soul."

4. Thomas Merton, quoted in Terry Tastard, *The Spark in the Soul* (New York: Paulist Press, 1989), 98.

5. Stephen J. Nichols, *Jonathan Edwards: A Guided Tour of His Life and Thought* (Phillipsburg, N.J.: P&R Publishers, 2001), 107.

6. Henri J. M. Nouwen, *Intimacy: Pastoral Psychological Essays* (Notre Dame, Ind.: Fides/Claretian, 1969), 23.

Chapter 5 - From Milk to Meat

1. Jack Handey, *Deep Thoughts* (New York: Berkley, 1992).

2. George Gordon Coulton, *The Medieval Village* (New York: Dover, 1989), 268.

3. Wilton Bunch, professor of divinity, Beeson Divinity School, Birmingham, Alabama.

4. A. W. Tozer, *The Knowledge of the Holy* (New York: HarperSanFrancisco, 1961), 1.

Chapter 6 - Hollow Places

1. Pliny, *The Letters of the Younger Pliny*, Betty Radice, trans. (London: Penguin, 1963), 171.

2. Ibid., 172.

3. Maria Antonietta Lozzi Bonaventura, *Pompeii, Herculaneum, Villa Jovis on Capri* (Rome: Editrice Millenium, 2002), 6.

4. Wilhelmina F. Jashemski, *The Gardens of Pompeii: Herculaneum and the Villas Destroyed by Vesuvius* (New York: Caratzas, 1979), 243.

5. *Day by Day We Magnify Thee: Daily Readings for the Church Year Selected from the Writings of Martin Luther*, Margarete Steiner, trans. (Philadelphia: Fortress, 1982), 108.

6. Jashemski, *The Gardens of Pompeii*, 8.

Chapter 7–Sushi Faith

1. C. S. Lewis, *The Four Loves* (London: Harcourt Brace & Company, 1960), 65.

2. Robb Walsh, "Raw Talent," *Houston Press*, 10 January 2002; on the Internet at www.houstonpress.com.

3. As quoted on the Internet at www.stanford.edu/group/King//

4. Charles Wesley, "And Can It Be?" *Baptist Hymnal* (Nashville: Convention Press, 1991), 147.

5. Keith Getty and Stuart Townsend, "In Christ Alone," © 2001 Kingsway Thank You Music. Used by permission.

6. Francois Fénelon, quoted in Richard J. Foster and James Bryan Smith, *Devotional Classics* (New York: HarperSanFrancisco, 1989), 47.

7. John Bunyan, *Grace Abounding to the Chief of Sinners* (Grand Rapids: Baker, 1978), 96.

8. Martin Luther, quoted in Richard J. Foster and Emilie Griffin, *Spiritual Classics* (New York: HarperSanFrancisco, 2000), 122.

Chapter 8–Blue Enough

1. Giles Oakley, *The Devil's Music: A History of the Blues* (New York: Harvest, 1976), 17.

2. Ibid., 37.

3. Ibid., 33.

4. Austin Sonnier Jr., *A Guide to the Blues* (Westport, Conn.: Greenwood), xiv.

5. Ibid., 1.

6. *Blues and Gospel Music*, Allan Moore, ed. (Cambridge, England: Cambridge Univ. Press, 2002), 63.

7. *Payday Someday: And Other Sermons by Robert Greene Lee* Timothy and Denise George, eds., (Nashville: Broadman and Holman, 1995), 246.

8. *The Valley of Vision: A Collection of Puritan Prayers & Devotions*, Arthur Bennett, ed. (Carlisle, Pa: Banner of Truth Trust, 2003), xxiv–xxv.

9. George, *Payday Someday*, 245–46.

Chapter 9 – A Gory Gospel

1. C. S. Lewis, *Grief* (Nashville: Nelson, 1998), 34.

2. Civilla D. Martin, "His Eye Is on the Sparrow," in *African American Heritage Hymnal* (Chicago: GIA Publications, Inc., 2001); in public domain.

3. Radu Florescu and Raymond T. McNally, *Dracula: A Biography of Vlad the Impaler 1431–1476* (New York: Hawthorn, 1973), 9.

4. Ibid., 37.

5. Pierre Barbet, M.D., *A Doctor at Calvary: The Passion of Our Lord Jesus Christ as Described by a Surgeon* (New York: Image Books, 1963), 119.

6. Examples include Job's sons and daughters, who were killed because of their debauchery (Job 1:18-19); the cities of Sodom and Gomorrah destroyed for their immorality (Genesis 19:24); and Ananias and his wife, who were killed for their deception (Acts 5:5-10).

7. Tom Beaudoin, *Virtual Faith: The Irreverent Spiritual Quest of Generation X* (San Fransciso: Jossey-Bass, 2000).

8. Many thanks to Mark Gignilliat, assistant professor of divinity at Beeson Divinity School, for reminding me of this truth.

9. "His Eye Is on the Sparrow," refrain.

10. Raymond T. McNally and Radu Florescu, *In Search of Dracula* (Greenwich, Conn.: New York Graphic Society, 1972), 102.

11. Ibid., 109.

12. Florescu and McNally, *Dracula*, 121.

13. Robert Lowry, "Nothing but the Blood;" in public domain.

Chapter 10 – Good Hamster Fluffy

1. Ray Robinson, *Famous Last Words* (New York: Workman, 2003), 31.

2. George Melvyn Ella, *William Cowper: Poet of Paradise* (Durham, England: Evangelical Press, 1993), 567.

3. George Melvyn Ella, *William Cowper: The Man of God's Stamp* (Dundas, Ontario: Joshua Press, 2000), 152.

4. Ella, *William Cowper: Poet*, 186.

5. Ibid.

6. Ella, *William Cowper: The Man*, 80.

7. Ibid., 81.

8. Ibid., 83.

9. William Cowper, "God Moves in a Mysterious Way," *Baptist Hymnal* (Nashville: Convention Press, 1991), 73; in public domain.

Chapter 11–Grappling with God

1. Random e-mail forwarded to the author.

2. As quoted in Joy Davidman, *Smoke on the Mountain* (1963; repr., Louisville, Ky.; Westminster, John Knox, 1985), foreword.

3. Paul Plass, *The Game of Death in Ancient Rome* (Madison, Wisc.: Univ. of Wisconsin Press, 1995), 53.

4. *Josephus: Complete Works*, William Whiston, trans. (Grand Rapids: Kregel, 1960), 657.

5. Stephen Turnbull, *The Samurai* (Tokyo: Japan Library, 1999), 137.

6. *Code of the Samurai*, Thomas Cleary, trans., (Tokyo: Tuttle Publishing, 1999), x.

7. Turnbull, *The Samurai*, 137–138.

8. Cleary, *Code of the Samurai*, 3.

9. David Beckham is a star soccer player for the England national team and has played professionally for Manchester (U.K.) United, Real Madrid, and most recently, the Los Angeles Galaxy.

Chapter 12–Back to the Future

1. C. S. Lewis, *The Weight of Glory* (New York: HarperSanFancisco, 1949; repr. HarperCollins 2001), 26.

2. Francis of Assisi, "All Creatures of Our God and King," *Baptist Hymnal* (Nashville: Convention Press, 1991), 27; emphasis added.

3. Philip Jenkins, *The Next Christendom* (Oxford, England: Oxford Univ. Press, 2007), 12.

4. Gerald Bray, research professor, Beeson Divinity School, Birmingham, Alabama.